PIVOT
&GO

www.amplifypublishing.com

Pivot & Go: The 29-Day Blueprint to Redefine and Achieve YOUR Success

I have tried to recreate events, locales, and conversations from my memories of them. In order to maintain their anonymity, in some instances I have changed the names of individuals and places. I may have changed some identifying characteristics and details such as physical properties, occupations, and places of residence.

For more information, please contact:
Amplify Publishing
620 Herndon Parkway #320
Herndon, VA 20170
info@amplifypublishing.com

Library of Congress Control Number: 2020900223

CPSIA Code: PRFRE0520A
ISBN-13: 978-1-64543-111-4

Printed in Canada

To my wife Taylor, I fall more and more in love with you every day.

To my future kids, may your eyes be open and set on the true joy of life—serving others.

PIV &

**The 29-Day Blueprint
to Redefine and
Achieve YOUR Success**

DAVID
NURSE

NBA Life Optimization Coach

amplify

CONTENTS

Foreword: Jeremy Lin..IX

Foreword: Taylor Kalupa...X

Introduction 1

Pregame: FAQ...9

Foundational Pivot 15

Day 1: Snapback Hats & Voting Ballots 24

Day 2: The Rich Life 34

Day 3: The 18th Second.. 44

Day 4: Cold Calls 54

Day 5: $120,000 Below Mount Everest........................... 64

Day 6: Harlem Globetrotters, Swedish Meatballs,
& Great White Shark Diving 72

Day 7: High Stakes Poker & Sushi in Cleveland............... 82

Day 8: Russian 'Kung-Fu' Master Lost
in the Streets of Brazil.. 90

Day 9: Balancing 52.3 Pounds of Sugar.......................... 102

Day 10: *The Best Cruise You'll Never Remember* 112

Day 11: *Foggy Mirrors* 122

Day 12: *Shooting Lessons with Mark Cuban* 130

Day 13: *Puzzle Piece Problems* 140

Day 14: *The Beach Front Patio* 152

Day 15: *Pizza Time* 160

Day 16: *The 82.5 Pound Stone on the Bottom of the Ocean* 168

Day 17: *Championship Souvlakis* 176

Day 18: *Multi-Millionaire Minion* 186

Day 19: *Listen to the Lyrics* 194

Day 20: *Board Game Changer* 204

Day 21: *Check This Off!* 210

Day 22: *Sodom's Apple* 218

Day 23: *Turtle Life* 228

Day 24: *Scrubbing Feces & Running Barefoot* 234

Day 25: *A 98 mph Fastball & a Fifth of Vodka* 244

Day 26: *The Greatest Ones You've Never Heard Of* 252

Day 27: *Younger You* 262

Day 28: *Congo to Hollywood* 270

Day 29+: *Relentless Consistency* 278

Acknowledgments 286

About the Author 288

FOREWORD
JEREMY LIN

I'M A BIG BELIEVER in pursuing your dreams regardless of what others or the world may say.

My life has been a myriad of overcoming obstacles and achieving things—through Christ—that everyone said were impossible.

We all have unique gifts and talents, but our personal fears and doubts are often our biggest limitations.

David is one of the most positive and joyful friends I have, and I'm glad he's shared all his secrets to personal success in this book.

If you want to pursue being the best you and pushing yourself to reach your highest potential, you will gain a lot from *Pivot & Go*!

FOREWORD
TAYLOR KALUPA

I GREW UP IN THE CITY OF DREAMS, lights, and Hollywood magic, a place that is home to some of the most successful and famous people in the world. As an actress, I have met and even worked with them. I'm humbled to say I was on a television series with the most SAG-nominated actress in history, Edie Falco; I have attended exclusive events with celebrities whose careers are inspiringly iconic, including Reese Witherspoon, Quentin Tarantino, Jennifer Aniston, and Leonardo DiCaprio, just to name a few. I was blessed to go to Pepperdine University, where I absorbed knowledge from one of the smartest and most experienced business school directors in the country.

I have spent my life surrounded by incredible, inspiring people. And in all my experiences, the person who stands out most is David Nurse.

Now, I know you might be thinking, *Well, of course he does! He's your husband and you love him.* And that's definitely true. But one of the reasons I fell in love with David was because he genuinely inspires me. His passion, joy, humble confidence, and enthusiasm for everything he does are magnetic. Truly, I have never met anyone as passionate about life as David.

I vividly remember the first day we met. I walked up to the Coffee Bean & Tea Leaf expecting to just meet a friend of a friend for a business meeting; a quick, professional favor. Little did I know, it was a set-up, and what started with an awkward half-hug/half-handshake in a coffee shop quickly turned into the best first date of my life. I could instantly tell that David was unapologetically himself in every area of his life, which gave him more confidence than I've ever seen, and in the humblest way you could imagine. As we sipped our coffees and walked along the beach for the next two hours, we talked about our careers, pasts, futures, and goals. Not once did David talk about what he had accomplished for himself. Instead, he beamed with excitement when he talked about other people's successes he aided in, about the love and joy he gets from spending time with his family and helping those in need, about the adventures he's been on and the many cultures he's experienced, and about his love for everyday life.

As I got to know him more, I learned just how well-traveled, intelligent, and truly successful he is. And yes, he is successful according to every worldly definition, but it's even more than that. David's success is much more deeply rooted. He truly doesn't worry about what others think, and he has a much bigger picture in mind. I remember the day that David told me he was turning down an NBA coaching job because he felt writing this book would allow him to help more people in the long run. He gave up an opportunity that he knew he would succeed at; one that everyone thought would be the potential pinnacle of his career. He risked falling completely on his face as he passionately engaged with a grueling writing process, a process completely out of his comfort zone. Watching him pursue his life goals of service and sacrifice to an entirely new standard caused me to pivot my own perspective of what success really means.

As you read this book, I want you to know that you are in the best hands possible. David changed my life completely. I know that if you are affected even 1 percent as much as I have been from knowing David, his outlook, his mindset, and his story, that will be more than enough to change your life forever. And I have a strong feeling this book will affect you just as much as it did me.

When David first asked me to look over his book, I thought, *Sure, I know everything there is to know about David, so this will be easy and quick.* Boy, was I wrong. As I dove into each chapter, I learned more about my husband than I would have ever expected. I had to stop and thank God that David is even still alive after reading about his worldly encounters, from being lost in the streets of Brazil to sleeping on random butchers' couches in Australia. There were times I cried, so in awe of how much he truly cares about helping others with this book. Reading about his life experiences, his interactions with others, and the lessons he learned that have made him the incredible person he is today, I grew more and more excited to read the next chapter. It made our marriage that much stronger and gave me insight into sides of David that I had never known.

Everyone has someone in their field of work or dream job that they aspire to be like. And everyone is obsessed with "the making of" documentaries that come out about the most successful or famous people. There's this urge to find the secret formula to getting to that place in life, a formula that will solve all of life's problems and make us who we want to be. You might doubt that such a formula exists. But I can honestly say that in this book, David has provided that formula. As excited as I have been to have my own personal successes in my career and throughout my life, I am even more excited for the world to read this book. I am more excited to be married to a man I know will change so many people's daily lives.

Regardless of what stage of life you are in, from fresh out of college to married with four kids, retired with grandchildren to interviewing for your first job, couch surfing while you find yourself to heading a multibillion dollar company, this book can, without a doubt, change your life. The power of perspective is the foundation of everything we do. It is the blueprint for life. And you have an innate desire to love this life you live. *Pivot & Go* gives you the tools to change your entire perspective on life! Buckle up, reader. You're in for an amazing ride!

INTRODUCTION

HEY, I'M DAVID NURSE, and I'm going to transform your life into something better than you can even imagine!

Today is your lucky day—it usually takes some work to get into my personal program. I'm on-the-go a lot and my roster is pretty full. I have coached more than 150 NBA players and many Fortune 500 CEOs. I am often called to speak as an expert in my craft; so far, I've hit over fifty countries and spanned six continents with my messages. I have set world records and grown a personal brand that is recognized worldwide. And now, I'm going to give you the formula I've used to accomplish everything so you can apply it to your own dreams.

No matter who you are or what you do, it's a formula YOU can use. No, really! I swear, I am nothing more than an average kid from the middle-of-nowhere cornfields of Iowa. I didn't attend a prestigious college. I wasn't given any preferential treatment growing up. I wasn't born into wealth—shoot, I didn't have a single dollar to my name until I was twenty-five. I wasn't born into great opportunity or with a world-altering talent or with above-average athleticism.

Even in my profession as a high-level life and optimization coach, I have no intensive certifications declaring my expertise. I am not a certified trainer. I don't have a background in sleep coaching, and I have never taken a mindfulness class in my life. I am not a scientist; I am not a doctor. I've never had a world-class gift for learning, I've never been in the top percent of my class (nowhere near!). I've never taken an IQ test for the sole reason that I don't care what it says. In short, there is nothing special about me.

There is, however, one thing that has made all the difference. It has made me who I am; it has helped me achieve everything. It has allowed me to rise to the top of my field, trumping every credential.

I have confidence. Confidence in who I am, in what I am doing, and in where I want to go. I am confident that I am in this exact spot right now for a reason and a purpose much larger than myself. I know I will achieve what I want if I work at it with relentless consistency, regardless of the obstacles I'm up against. Unwavering confidence and belief in myself have carried me every step of the way.

If I can achieve all of my dreams and more and live exactly the life I want, it's an *absolute fact* that you can, too.

See, my dream from day one was to play in the NBA. Scratch that, it wasn't just my dream—it was my everything. My earliest childhood memory was my first day of preschool. I can remember two things vividly—seeing my mom cry as she drove away and seeing a basketball hoop in the corner of the room, which quickly wiped any thoughts of missing my mom. All through elementary school, I wore a basketball jersey, usually the same one the entire week. (I really liked the reversible jerseys; I thought I could fool everyone into thinking I'd changed.)

Basketball is in my blood. My uncle played high-level Division 1 college basketball before going professional internationally, and then became a professional coach. I was determined to be just like him, except I would one-up him and play in the NBA. The whole blueprint of my life was laid out in front of me from a very young age. I was set.

Fast forward to my senior year of college, and one question began to sink its teeth into me everywhere I turned: "What are you doing after college?"

"The NBA."

I kept getting chuckles followed by, "No, really, what are you going to do when you graduate?"

Everything I'd done was focused around making it to the NBA—there was no back-up plan. None.

Only then did I start to see the writing on the wall—the NBA didn't have many 6'2", white, unathletic players in the league. At the time, it was Steve Nash and . . . well, yeah, that was about it. As my college career ended, no agents came calling and no NBA draft boards had me on them (or anywhere close, for that matter). I was not going to play in the NBA. The realization stung bad. The thing I had worked my entire life for, the plan from my first memory, was swept out from under me.

Fortunately, though, my uncle was the head coach of an NBA D-League team (the level directly below the NBA, which actually fed players to the NBA). If he drafted me, I would still have a chance!

I did my best sales pitch, and he drafted me in the eighth and final round to the Iowa Energy. My uncle wanted the best for me— he was a mentor and an older brother figure who always looked out for me. Now we could live together while I played for his team and worked my way up to the NBA. Life plan back on track.

Training camp was tough—REALLY tough. But I was able to hold my own against the best players on the team. What I didn't have in God-given talent, I made up for in grit and toughness. I was a blue-collar player with a good-looking jump shot; in my mind, however, I was a lot better. I was going to be the star.

My uncle had other opinions. I got released at the end of training camp. *I didn't make the team.* I couldn't make the team that my own uncle coached, in a league below the one I had dreamed of playing in my whole life. I was crushed.

My uncle, still looking out for me, connected me with his good friend in Australia. This guy was the last word in Australian basketball—if he told teams to take me, they would listen. Without seeing me in person or even seeing film on me, the West Adelaide Bearcats of Adelaide, Australia welcomed me onto their team.

To get a good concept of international basketball, throw every NBA vision that you have out the window and replace it with something closer to a circus. All of my teammates worked other jobs; basketball was literally their hobby. For everyone else, the West Adelaide Bearcats was a great way to get together with friends on the weekend and have a beer—before, during, and after the game.

It was not a good environment for me, someone who lived and breathed basketball and spent every waking hour in the gym. I was rocked, extremely wounded, and my confidence was at an all-time low. I'd put so much work into this; why couldn't I be as good as I wanted to be? Why wasn't I better than this? It didn't make sense to me.

The saving grace was knowing I'd do summer basketball camps with my uncle all over the Midwest when my season was finished. I would be close to "real" basketball and near my role model and mentor again.

The summer was great. My uncle and I didn't miss a beat; we were best friends growing a business that had the vision and potential to be something very big. I was happy to work for him. I didn't care about the money; I was just excited to grow something lasting together. He gave me encouragement and motivation and vowed to help me get another shot overseas—this time, in his old European stomping grounds.

He delivered, setting me up to play in one of the top basketball countries in the world, Spain. Life was back on track: I would have a long and successful basketball career in Europe (the second-best league behind the NBA). If I couldn't have the NBA, well, at least I would be able to see other cultures, travel the world, and play the game I loved at a very high level. Maybe this was actually meant for me all along.

I had a few late August basketball camps lined up to run for my uncle in Iowa before heading off to Spain. However, as fate and European basketball would have it, they wanted me over there earlier than we had previously arranged in the contract (a contract that paid me just enough to eat baguettes and maybe a tapa or two each day in the Northern Basque region). Young and immature, I decided it was best to just hide my dilemma from my uncle. So, I hired someone else to run the camp. Summer camps would finish, I'd be in Spain, and my uncle would be happy—life would be good.

Except the person I hired to run the camp was the wrong person. The completely wrong person. (Life lesson: know a person inside and out before hiring them to be in charge of a very important task.) The camp was a disaster, and I was halfway across the world receiving calls, emails, and texts from basically every parent, demanding their money back. And of course, my uncle was receiving them, too.

It tore us apart. It was on me, completely, as much as I didn't want to admit it. And I felt the wrath—my best friend/role model/ mentor no longer even spoke to me.

Right when I thought I had found a new life, I was suddenly alone in the deep mountains of a small Basque village. No one spoke English; hardly anyone even spoke Spanish. Basque, a language I had absolutely no foundation in, was all I heard at practice and everywhere I went.

As depressed and sorry for myself as I was, I knew I could hold on to my one outlet, basketball. And I would use the fuel to fire my performance on court. Basketball could get me through it all; it was what I put every waking hour into, after all. It was my identity.

It didn't work out that way, but I don't want to ruin all the stories in the book—there's a lot to learn from them. I learned a lot of things the hard way, but you'll be able to learn them easier—in a way that is much more fun, entertaining, and flat-out life changing.

At age twenty-four, I had nothing. Literally nothing. But I chose a path, something that would separate me from everyone else. I made myself an expert and traveled all over the globe. Now, I have everything I ever dreamed of and more. But it took some changes to the way I thought about, experienced, and interacted with the world. Not major changes, just small pivots. Small *mindset pivots.*

What is a *mindset pivot?* It's seeing things from a different light, a different perspective. It is pivoting on our current positions, the ones that keep us stuck or drag us down, and moving towards the futures we so badly desire. It's redefining terms that we allow others to define for us—success, failure, joy, passion, confidence—and, in creating these new definitions, becoming the people we were made to be.

I wake up every morning with unlimited energy and enthusiasm—and you can, too. I can help you live every day with genuine joy, passion for what you do, and unprecedented confidence in who you are. This book gives you the ultimate formula to the life you want to live. Through twenty-nine days of mindset pivots, illustrated through impactful stories and life-altering daily activities, we will drag you out of any mud you're stuck in, out of any ruts, and on track to *thriving* instead of just *surviving.*

You already have the tools inside of you—you have been blessed with incredible gifts that only you possess, which, when used correctly, will allow you to live your ultimate life. No longer will you look around and see other people enjoying their lives and think "That's just for the lucky few." No, it's for YOU! And this book can get you there.

I say *can*, because the choice is up to you. The mindset pivots in this book work 1,000% of the time—but only if YOU want them to. If you fully embrace the blueprint, you will not only change your life, each and every one of your days will be better than the one before. You will find a daily rhythm that feels almost unfair, like a cheat code to life that you shouldn't have. You will feel almost guilty when your life seems too good to be true. You might even feel like you don't deserve it! You will wonder, "Why am I suddenly blessed with these outlooks? Why am I now able to live the amazing life I have always wanted to live?"

If you are perfectly fine with every aspect of your life, this book isn't for you. But if you want more out of life, if you want to be the person you were created to be, and if you want to live the life you have always dreamt of, this is EXACTLY the book for you!

Everything happens for a reason and a purpose. There is a reason you picked up this book, a reason you are reading it right now, and a reason you are going to turn to the next page, where you will start pivoting your routines and habits into something incredible. You will have an outlook on life that everyone envies, that everyone *wants* to have. You will share it with others through the way you live. It will be visible in the way you treat everyone around you, in the way you give, give, and give some more.

You'll know exactly what makes you YOU. And I am super excited for you!

PREGAME

FAQ

THE GENERAL CONCEPT OF THIS book is pretty simple: you read one day at a time, in order, enjoy the stories, learn the lessons, complete the activities, and watch your life change dramatically. In twenty-nine days, you'll be living a better life than you can imagine at this moment, and that crazy momentum just keeps compounding. Not a bad deal, right?

Before we dive in, I'm taking a moment to answer a few common questions so I can set you up for *your* best success.

What the heck? Why twenty-nine days?

There are a ton of studies that show it takes twenty-eight days to develop a habit. (Some say twenty-one—I tend to think that's too short. Others insist it's sixty-six—that's way too much. In sixty-six days, you'll already be well into living your new life!) Through all of my experience, twenty-eight days is just about right.

Habits can be built in twenty-eight days, but *lifestyle* comes on day 29. And every day after. By completing all twenty-nine days, you'll have the habits you need integrated into the full framework in order to sustain the lifestyle.

How am I supposed to read this book?
What are all these categories?

This book is broken down day by day—you never have to read any further than the day you're on. Each day fits into our five main mindset categories: **Success, Failure, Joy, Passion,** and **Confidence.** Master these five, and you've got it all.

But there's a catch.

They are *not* what the world wants you to believe they are. I could tell you right now how they need to be redefined to pivot your entire life. But it just wouldn't be as effective. There is a big difference in *knowing vs. doing,* and the doing journey is one you've got to take for yourself. Day by day, you'll learn exactly what it is to redefine each of these terms and you'll see *exactly* why I didn't tell you right from the start. Trust me.

So, for now, here are the common and socially-accepted definitions, cribbed straight from Webster:

> **Success:** the gaining of wealth, respect, or fame
>
> **Failure:** neglect of an assigned or expected action: inability to perform a normal function well enough
>
> **Joy:** a feeling of great pleasure or happiness that comes from success, good fortune, or a sense of well-being
>
> **Passion:** strong feeling or emotion: great affection: an object of desire or deep interest
>
> **Confidence:** a feeling of trust or belief: a feeling of certainty

Now, promptly forget those. By the end of this book, you're going to be living much cooler definitions, one action step at a time.

I have placed the category markers in the margins of each day so that once you are finished the book, you can easily go back and brush up on any of the five sections as you need it. Working on the action steps found at the end of each chapter isn't a one-time shot either; you can continually go back to relearn and re-evaluate, which I highly encourage.

When should I start?

What's your favorite day of the week?

The majority of you will probably say Friday or Saturday, or maybe some of you workaholics out there love Mondays (okay, probably not). But the one day we all *love* doesn't actually show up on any calendar. It's the day most of us say we will get "it" done. It's the day when we'll find the time to get married to our longtime sweetheart. The day when we'll start a family and have kids. The day when we'll get the courage to ask out the babe behind the counter at our favorite restaurant, or the one in the office who always sneaks glances our way. The day when we will start eating healthier and implementing an exercise routine. The day we will take that trip to the mountains with our kids we've been putting off since we started our new job, or the bucket list adventure that we have always wanted to go on.

That day will come, we tell ourselves. It'll happen. "Someday." Someday, we'll follow our passion; we'll take a leap of faith and go after the goals we have set for ourselves. "Someday."

But "Someday" doesn't exist on the calendar, and it never will. And if we keep adding everything that we want to do to "Someday," none of it will ever happen. It will just continue to pile up. We will look back on it years from now with terrifying regret. "Someday" is an excuse we find a million different times to use.

There will never be a right time in life for anything. Get used to that. No one has lived the perfect life (other than Jesus). No one has the perfect timing for everything they do; it just doesn't happen that way and never will.

Today is the day to get busy living. "Someday" doesn't exist. You want to live the life you've always dreamed of living? It's all in the pages ahead of you. *Today* is your day to start. You've already started!

I find that each of these pivots works best in the morning; it helps set up your whole day before it even really gets going. But starting your morning off right begins before you even shut your eyes in the evening; in the next section, we're going to set up the evening and morning routine you should start tonight, so that you can tackle day 1 first thing tomorrow morning!

What if I'm not up to the challenge?

There's a lot that goes into a twenty-nine-day challenge if you really think about it. A lot of different *mindset pivots*. First, you have to *actually* want to change. (But you wouldn't be this far in the book if that wasn't the case. Remember, you picked this book up for a reason and a purpose!)

You have a special superhero power inside of you. Not the "save burning buildings" or "fly to distant lands" type. This superhero power isn't just for the lucky few or the ultra-talented or those born into wealth. That superhero power is *choice.*

You have power in every single choice you make. You can *choose* how you view each and every one of your days—how you start it, how you spend it, whom you spend it with, and how you end it. Endless choices.

You can absolutely build the foundation for the life you have always wanted to live. The power is in you; the decision is whether you want to use it and become the person you were made to be, or suppress it and go along with whatever society tells you that you *have* to be. This mindset is yours. The choice is yours. You're up for the challenge as long as you *choose* to be up for the challenge.

Making the choice to use this superhero power can seem daunting, but I'm here for you. That's why we're going to take our time over the next twenty-nine days to make smaller choices, to explore the mindset pivots with more nuance, and to tackle the tough stuff in life one thing at a time. This way, you'll gain a new mindset each day that flows together perfectly with the days before it and the days following. It'll not only be painless—it'll actually be a lot of fun!

At this moment, you might think of yourself as someone who starts things but never finishes. Making changes can feel too hard, too daunting. You might just be working to survive to the next day. *If only I had time. If only I could get my to-do list done. If only exercising was fun. If only I could go back to my childhood.*

That was the old you.

This is the new you. The master of *mindset pivoting.* The superhero with everything at the tip of your pinkie. You aren't just up for this challenge—you were born for it. This book is just the permission to pivot you've been waiting for—so let's GO!

FOUNDATIONAL PIVOT

To INCREASE YOUR SUCCESS FROM the very first minute, there are two simple foundations you can build on. These staple routines build and shape your days, beginning from the moment you wake up and ending the moment you shut your eyes and drift off to sleep. Your morning and nightly routines sandwich together the meat of the day, which always has the potential to be the best *or* worst of your life. It all comes down to your perception and perspective, and building the base for those starts with these routines.

Try this on for size:

The aroma and steam of your warm cup of coffee lift up into the morning sky while you sit peacefully, looking off into the distance at the sun rising and the waves gently crashing into the shore. You take deep breaths in and long, slow breaths out, feeling every rise and fall in your chest. The sound of birds chirping fills the air. You take another sip of your coffee and wonder how you got this great life. What have you done to deserve this perfect, beautiful morning?

Okay, now this one:

The alarm blares in your ear only slightly louder than the TV news updates, variations of the crimes and tragedies you fell asleep watching the night before. Groggy and still exhausted, you roll over to check your phone. You scowl as you scroll through the seemingly perfect snapshots on your social media feed (why does everyone else's life look so awesome?). You check your notifications to find fourteen unread messages, twelve new emails, and three missed calls waiting. Your mind races—*what do all these people want, it's a Saturday morning?!?*

You stumble out of bed and run over to the coffee maker. You're down to one coffee pod, your least favorite flavor in the wholly unsatisfying variety pack you grabbed in your grocery-store rush. The unmade bed and sink full of dirty dishes taunt you, but you don't have time to make those right. As you force down your less-than-enjoyable cup of coffee, you flip open your laptop and begin responding to your messages and emails, hoping that your on-the-fly guesses at priority are correct. Your inbox fills more rapidly than you can clear it. You catch the clock at the top corner of your screen—it's 6:38 AM.

You pause for a second and wonder how you got here. When did this *rat race* become your life? How does every morning turn into something so intense, more frenetic than putting out a skyscraper fire?

Which scenario do you want?

Number one, right? Of course, because that is what a morning *should be like*—peaceful, inspiring gratitude, and exactly the way YOU want it to be. We shouldn't spend our mornings tied to phones, laptops, and lists of *ultra-important* things that we won't even remember we did a week later.

So . . . why do you keep choosing option two?

It's easy to slip into the second mode, checking your phone before you even peel both eyes open and allowing your mind to race in a million different directions at a million miles per hour. But this mode swallows you up, robs you of your daily joy, and puts you in a position that is almost impossible to bounce back from.

Everyone talks about the importance of morning routines. Lists of "lifehacks" designed to make you more efficient are trendy. But your morning routine is so much more than what you can accomplish in your first waking moments. Before you throw yourself into a never-ending to-do list, you need to conquer the *mindset pivot* of the routine.

Routines make us who we are. They shape our entire days; they shape our lives. People who don't make conscious choices about their routines are just welcoming constant anxiety and uncertainty. They allow their days to dominate them from the moment they wake up.

The choices you make and the actions you take during your morning routine establish the mindset that will, in turn, shape your entire day. And over the course of 365 mornings a year and 7,300 mornings over the next twenty years, the consistency of the mindset you establish each morning determines how your life will be lived, whether you realize it or not.

The *mindset pivot* begins with identifying how you look at your morning. Do you see it as a sacred time to be protected? An opportunity to fully breathe in the amazing gift of life? Is it the chance to enjoy your favorite cup of coffee, to peacefully sit in silence, free of any burden or worry? Or do you hit the snooze button six more times because you dread waking up to the life you've built?

The mindset you need to lay the foundation for your ultimate life is clear. Now, you just need to *choose* it, which begins with establishing routines that make this choice second nature.

Jumpstart Your Morning

Yes, every morning is a fresh start to a brand-new day—but who you are when you wake up is closely tied to who you were when you fell asleep. It's hard to wake up fresh and positive if you fell asleep stressed and depressed. It is extremely overlooked, but how you finish your day actually *matters.*

Think about it—when you finish anything in life on a positive note, aren't you more fired up and motivated to attack that thing again the next time? Don't you bring that feeling of success and accomplishment into your next venture? If you finish a guitar lesson strumming chords you have never been able to play before, you're chomping at the bit to rock out and learn more in the next session. If you finish a snowboarding lesson shredding the slopes, you're juiced up for your next trip to the mountains. If you have an awesome day at work, you bring that positive vibe back home to your spouse and kids and into your next day of work.

Point being, if you finish your day in a joyful state of mind, you wake up the next day still in that positive mindset. Instead of pulling the covers over your head and hitting the snooze button, you're more inclined to pop out of bed, more motivated to continue on the exciting path ahead of you. You don't just *face* the day ahead—you *embrace* the day ahead.

I'm going to share my nightly and morning routines with you, but I want to make a few things very clear. First, this is simply the best recipe I've devised for myself—I know yours will be different, tailored to your needs. I'm sure even mine will continue to change and evolve. I've built this routine from lots of trial and error and research into the best practices I could find. Second, it might look a little overwhelming—don't think yours needs to be as involved, especially at first! There are exceptions to every routine—unforeseen circumstances creep up, emergencies take priority, and travel shifts the details of everyday life. For example, if one of my NBA players is playing an important night game, I'll adjust my standard routine to stay up later and give them a post-game congratulations. If I don't do every step in my routine, I DON'T BEAT MYSELF UP FOR IT! Even if I do something completely counter to one of my steps, I don't think twice about it. I know the best decision I can make is the *next* decision I make, and I'm right back up on that horse.

My Nightly Routine

1. The **UNWIND:** There is a time each day when we *need* to shut off. Call it closing up shop, call it logging out, call it "calling it"—just, whatever you do, stop picking up that phone.

I can hear you groaning. Look, I get it. I'm super Type A. I go, go, go to the max, and I'm always making moves to get ahead. We have the technology to be "on" 24/7, but if you try to fire on all cylinders at all hours, you will crash and burn out. Every day has to end; rather than spending my last ounce of energy firing another tweet into the void or checking my email one last time, I choose to consciously end my "working" day.

When I am back at my apartment and I've put in a solid day's work, I tell myself, "David, you did good today. Good on you, mate." (I like using the slang—it lightens up the mood and makes me feel like I'm back in Australia.) Then I put my phone on silent and I tuck it in an inconvenient corner of the living room so I'm not tempted to constantly check it.

Divorcing myself from my phone each night mentally shuts down my rat-race brain from the things I could still get done and those I will need to do tomorrow. I highly recommend it. Whatever you choose, find a way to tell yourself and the world that the business day is done so that you can move into . . .

2. The ENJOYMENT: This stage is all about focusing on enjoyment and being *fully present*. Not being fully present when you're doing something enjoyable (like an activity with your kids or spending time with your significant other) because you feel like you need to "get ahead" is inexcusable. It causes stress, depression, and long-term joylessness. When you're not fully present, you can't fully enjoy what you're doing.

For me, there is nothing better than cooking a nice, healthy, gourmet dinner with my wife, praying and giving thanks, and enjoying a movie, sporting event, or even looking back through old wedding pictures. No way would I not be fully engaged for that!

3. The BEAUTY SLEEP: Step three is the most obvious and the most critical—but we cheat ourselves of a good night's sleep all the time. Trust me, sleep is not for the weak, sleep is for the *smart and wise*! Working with some of the world's top athletes, I have learned tools for optimizing shut-eye from the best sleep coaches in the world.

To ensure I get a great night's rest, I . . .

> **Mind Dump:** In my journal, I write down anything on my mind or anything that I need to do the next day and then give myself permission to stop thinking about those until after my morning routine.

> **Eight Hour Myth:** I assure myself that I am going to wake up rested and ready to attack the next day, no matter how many hours I sleep. If I get eight hours, awesome! If I get six, it'll be fine—I'll just build a fifteen-minute nap into my schedule, and that will recharge me and get me ready for . . .

My Morning Routine

1. I get up at a slow, pleasant pace, make my bed and turn on soft worship/praise music.

2. Grind my own coffee beans and make my favorite style of coffee in my Chemex.

3. Sit outside (or if it's too cold, in my favorite comfy chair), watching the sunrise and spending time in grateful reflection. I journal about things I am thankful and excited for, a small joy that happened the previous day, things I want to keep working on, and three people I am going to text or call. I end my quiet morning reflection time by reading a morning devotional that helps me grow deeper in my relationship with Christ.

4. Perform some light stretching and roll out on a softball (to break up the fascia and any muscle soreness) while listening to a podcast or audiobook on something I want to learn more about.

5. Take a three-minute ice cold shower to jumpstart my body and mentally prep to absolutely attack the day!

6. I write down three things I am going to accomplish for the day. These can range from business growth to meeting with someone to something I want to learn—anything that moves the needle forward and helps me become the best version of myself.

7. Lastly, I read all the *mindset pivot* notecards (you'll have these soon, too) placed around my house. All of them.

On the days I am able to hit each one of these, I start off knowing I am in the absolute best state of mind I can possibly be in. I have already won my day, because I have won my morning.

Imagine nights that genuinely refresh you and end every day on a positive, joyful note. Imagine mornings you're rested and energetically excited to start. It's an amazing feeling to be in control of your mornings and evenings. It's time to pivot your morning and evening mindset and find the blueprint that brings you closer to living out your *ultimate* day, every day. If you conquer this step, the next twenty-nine days will be a breeze!

BLUEPRINT ACTION PLANS

1. Identify how you see your mornings and evenings and what changes in your perceptions you need to consciously tackle to win the day.

2. Write out your perfect morning. What does it look like? How do you end your day to prep for it? How do you wake up? What beautiful things are you grateful for, and how could you engage with them to set the tone for your day?

3. Break down your description into an easy-to-implement, actionable daily routine. Feel free to take my routine and mold it to fit you perfectly!

4. Take the sheet of paper with your morning routine and place it in the spot you'd normally place your phone before bed. Now, instead of reaching and grabbing your phone first thing in the morning, you'll grab this piece of paper—the blueprint for your perfect morning.

DAY 1

SNAPBACK HATS & VOTING BALLOTS

YOU KNOW, I'M NOT A HAT GUY. I'm more into headbands. I've got a Lululemon headband that just feels right—gives me the swag I want out on the court when I'm training NBA players. When I put it on, I know I've got my mojo flowing, and that gives me confidence in myself. It's my style; it's who *I am*.

Basketball players don't really wear hats when they're playing and working out. Seeing the basket is a pretty crucial element of the game, of course, so anything that obstructs their view isn't ideal. Seems intuitive. In fact, over all my years of running basketball camps and coaching, I think I've only ever had to tell one kid to take off his baseball cap while playing

But then Kelly Olynyk, multi-millionaire NBA star, started showing up to workouts every single day in a backwards snapback with his hair flowing out underneath. Whether it was sweaty from the day before or a fresh new cap, his hat-of-the-day stayed on the entire workout. (In four months, I saw it fall off once. Yep, once. Until I saw it fall off, I actually thought it might be glued to his head somehow.)

I started to notice a trend: whatever hat Kelly chose, that was the type of player he was that day. If it was a Gonzaga hat, you were sure to hear stories of his college days; he even seemed to play more like he had in college, basically doing whatever he wanted on the basketball court with complete freedom and peace. If it was the Miami Heat hat (his current NBA team), he would be focused on the upcoming season, from the way he talked about what he needed to improve on to how professionally he approached the game.

But the best hat, my favorite hat of all, was the one that simply read *SWAG*.

I saw the SWAG hat and met Kelly-the-SWAG-player for the first time on a sticky hot mid-July morning at 7:55 AM on the dot. Kelly (one of the few NBA players who always shows up earlier than scheduled) strolled in wearing his cutoff sweatpant shorts, Miami Heat tank top, and the hat. By 7:56, he was ready to go—shoes on, hat snapped in, there to work. (Kelly is also one of the very rare breed of athletes who doesn't need to warm up at all.)

As the workout progressed, I noticed an extra bounce in his step, an extra sense of something . . . well, *extra*. Shot after shot, bottom of the net. Gracefully flowing up and down the court, huge smile on his face, doing literally whatever he wanted in the pick-up games. Some of the best NBA players, names and talent that would make your jaw drop, were in the gym that day, too. Yet, Kelly totally dominated. And it all seemed so effortless for him.

Kelly is unique, to say the least. You won't find anyone else like him in professional basketball. At seven years old, he told his father he would play in the NBA. Only problem? He was short—really short. As a junior in high school, he was 6'3", less than athletic, and a skilled but not dominant point guard.

Just another one of many fish in the basketball sea. Until he hit a growth spurt—a seven-inch growth spurt. Suddenly, he was 6'10" with the skills of a guard. Trust me, that versatility made colleges and NBA scouts drool.

But this new height came with some new challenges. He became extremely clumsy and jeans just didn't fit him anymore. Socially, he was a little bit awkward (and in high school, as we all remember, fitting in is everything). People throughout his hometown would point at him and gawk like he was a circus spectacle. For a sixteen-year-old kid, that's a heavy burden to bear.

That's when Kelly started wearing the hats.

Under the hats, he became a new person. He wasn't afraid of what others thought of him; he didn't have to try to fit in. Under the hats, Kelly was confident and free. He was voting for himself when he picked out his daily hat: *he* decided who he was going to be that day, without caring what anyone else thought.

At the same age that Kelly was telling his father he'd be joining the NBA—an age that most of us dedicate to incredibly tough life decisions like whether we want mac and cheese or Pop-Tarts for lunch—Rashon had different responsibilities. By seven years old, he was helping his mom put food on the table for his siblings. By eight, both his parents had passed. Rashon was the head of the household, called to protect his siblings as they struggled to make it from one day to the next in the projects of New Jersey, with gunshots, heroin, and cocaine right outside their door.

Blessed by the charity and help of some very gracious people in his life, Rashon was able to attend high school. However, before he graduated, he suffered yet another devastating loss: He had to bury his sister, whom he was extremely close to. Life didn't just throw curveballs at Rashon; it threw the entire kitchen sink, dishwasher and dryer at him before he even reached adulthood.

Through all the difficult times, Rashon would repeat to himself, "I am whatever I want to be." He would say it out loud, walking through the streets while praying a bullet wouldn't come his way. He would say it before he went to bed, after making sure his siblings were fed and had a warm place to sleep. In doing so, he was constantly *voting for himself.*

Rashon was a smaller-than-average kid with pretty huge dreams and aspirations. Somehow, amidst all the pain and struggle, he was able to see a ray of hope. Rashon decided college basketball was the ticket out of his current life and into the better one he desired. The problem was that, being 5'7" and 150 pounds soaking wet, he didn't look anything like a basketball player. College coaches didn't walk through the doors of his high school enamored by his potential.

But Rashon didn't care. He had been through everything and then some. There was no way he was going to let height stand in the way of his dreams. Every day, he would tell himself, "I *am* going to be a college basketball player and I *am* going to get a scholarship." When you're a 5'7" basketball player, there is really only one way to bring a lot of value to a team: mastering defense. And Rashon brought it like the junkyard bulldog that he was, turning himself into one of the top defenders in the country.

His high school coach was no slouch either—he was, in fact, something of a legend. Bob Hurley didn't just pour into Rashon on the court; he took him under his wing and built Rashon up to be a leader. Bob *voted* daily for Rashon and, in turn, helped Rashon *vote* daily for himself.

And Rashon made it. DePaul University gave him a full ride scholarship to play the game he loved. Not only did he *survive*, he *thrived*. He became a three-time team captain and one of the greatest players to ever wear a DePaul uniform.

After college, Rashon turned his eye towards business. He viewed money as the only guarantee that he would live a happy life and never face the struggles of his childhood again. Despite the fact that society considered him below-average intellectually, he voted for himself to become a rich businessman. He entered the corporate world, and those daily ballots won—he made great money.

Unfortunately, everything he earned and accomplished in the business world didn't satisfy Rashon. He was empty inside; he wasn't living out his passion. As much as he wanted the money to give him purpose, he knew, deep down, it never would.

Then, one cold night in the windy city of Chicago, Rashon turned on *Friday Night Lights*. Watching TV was the closest he got to the game of basketball, sports, or anything associated with that life anymore.

But that evening, something changed. Watching the coach on this fictional show passionately lead his team onto the football field, watching him exemplify servanthood by pouring into each individual player, well, it triggered something in Rashon. This passionate, caring, selfless, and genuinely giving character reminded him so much of his high school coach, Bob Hurley Sr. He decided the world needed to know that there was a real man just as incredible as this fictional TV hero.

So, Rashon cast another ballot for himself—he now voted for himself to become an executive film producer, so that he could make a film to share the story of the coach who'd given him everything. He had no experience at all in film, but he decided to give up his position in the business world to pursue the person he'd decided to become next. As Rashon would say, "I am whatever I want to be."

PBS picked up the film, and *The Street Stops Here* became one of the most watched documentaries of the year (and continues to be one of the most watched sports documentaries to this day). Now, if you say the name Bob Hurley Sr. to anyone in the basketball world, they know exactly who you are talking about—all because of Rashon's documentary.

Sure, that's a feel-good story, but it doesn't end there. Through making this film and seeing the joyful impact his high school coach had on everyone around him, Rashon was called to do the same. He wanted to be a basketball coach—and not just a high school basketball coach. He wanted to coach the highest level of college basketball. "I am whatever I want to be." Rashon voted yet again for himself.

Rashon started all over in yet another field that wasn't exactly easy to break into. He began with a high school coaching job and quickly rose to the college coaching level he wanted; then, just as quickly, he was fired. While a lot of people would have taken that as a sign that it wasn't meant to be and given up, Rashon picked himself up and got right back to it. He started again at square one as a high school coach, consistently voted for himself daily, and slowly climbed to his ultimate goal. Rashon is currently the associate head coach for the Arizona State Sun Devils. The head coach? Bob Hurley Jr.

Rashon did it—he risked starting completely over, multiple times in multiple fields, in order to pursue each of his passions. He never let the assumptions of the outside world dictate how he viewed himself nor what he believed he could accomplish. He pursued every passion with everything he had. Because he believed in himself and relentlessly voted for himself daily, Rashon won each of those self-elections with such landslide results that the rest of the world had no other choice than to agree. "I am who I want to be" translated to the rest of the world as "He is who he wants to be."

Rashon has become a close friend of mine over the years. He didn't tell me his story the first day we met; it took me six months to pry it out of him. He doesn't like to glorify himself; he only wants to point to others and pour into them.

Kelly does it with hats. Rashon does it with verbal self-affirmations. It doesn't matter how you do it. Just pick the voting tactic that works best for you and understand that you are able to choose *exactly* who you want to be, *every single day*. That's your superhero power, after all—CHOICE!

I was never a writer before this book, not even close. I despised writing papers in college. If you'd said, "David Nurse, the author" to anyone who knows me, they would have laughed (probably hysterically) and told you that you had the wrong guy: "No, you mean David Nurse, the NBA shooting coach."

And rightfully so. That's *exactly* the vote I'd cast for myself every morning for nearly seven years. That's the only hat (well, Lululemon headband) I wore for the world. "David Nurse" and "basketball" were married. (They still are, but let's just say it's more of an open relationship now.) The word "author" would never have been associated with my name. Not in a million years! Until one day, I decided to put on a different hat.

After I decided I was going to write this book, I woke up every morning and voted for myself to be an author. I was now "David Nurse, the author." "David Nurse, NBA shooting coach" will always be with me, but it couldn't solely define me forever. I voted "author" in, and as you can see, I won in a landslide. Shoot, I even convinced you!

Just because society thinks of us as *something* doesn't mean we have to be that *something*. You certainly can't fault the world for reading the hat you're wearing; if you want people to read something else, change it up—pivot towards your passion.

I believe in finding joy in any circumstance, but we also have to recognize that we ARE what we voted for ourselves to become. If you hate the circumstance you're currently in, change your daily vote! The election doesn't happen overnight; it could even take a four-year term. But in the long run, that's a pretty short sacrifice to spend the rest of your life doing what you love.

BLUEPRINT ACTION PLAN

1. Inside the ballot, write down your name and who you want to become. For example, if you want to write a book, then you will be voting for yourself daily to be an *author*. If you want to make a movie, then you will be voting for yourself daily to be a *filmmaker*. Don't get hung up on all the steps and hurdles between you and that dream right now. Whatever your big dream is, write it in here!

   You by no means need to quit your job and drop everything to pursue it; just start working towards that goal by casting you "daily vote" and dedicating an hour or so each day to making your ballot a reality. Start telling yourself that's who you are, and start telling everyone around you that you've cast a new ballot.

2. Write down "I VOTE FOR MYSELF DAILY" on a notecard and place it next to the spot for your incoming and outgoing mail. Commit to reading it and reflecting on the ballot you've cast for yourself today each time you handle the mail. Say it aloud and stand proud—I couldn't believe how motivating it was to hear the words, "I'm David Nurse, the author," come out of my mouth each day!

★ VOTE ★

NAME:
_____

POSITION:
_____

NOTES:
_____
_____
_____
_____
_____
_____
_____

DAY 2
THE RICH LIFE

GROWING UP, I LOVED ANY book or movie where the main characters held up an old, ripped-to-shreds map with a faint red X marked somewhere deep in the jungle. That X—the treasure, the goal that justified the mission—brought the heroes riches, glory, fame, and everything they had ever wanted and dreamed of. X marked the spot.

A month after my professional basketball playing career ended abruptly in Spain, I decided I was done licking my wounds and living on the recliner in my parent's living room. I packed up my car and drove for twenty-eight hours, eventually landing in the guest room of my friend Kris' apartment in Oakland, California. Kris was just recently married, so a long-term houseguest was not exactly a dream come true for them. However, they were generous and I was desperate. I was wounded, depressed, and frantic to make a move. I honestly had no idea what I would do from there, but I figured any move that took me off that recliner was a move in the right direction.

Sitting on the guest room bed one foggy afternoon, I scrolled through my bank account on my computer and finally saw something that made me feel good: $1,322.

Now, prior to my move to Oakland, my net income from playing basketball overseas was barely enough to cover the one-way plane ticket back to the States. My life's dream, my mission, my purpose (or so I'd thought) had netted me about $322 total.

But I had just finished running my very first solo basketball camp. The check had cleared, and the results were green and crisp. I was rich: I had made a thousand dollars in one single day.

So, I thought, *if I run 100 camps a year, I can make $100,000. Calculate that by a factor of ten years—I can make one million dollars! If $1,000 feels this good when I'm hurting this bad, $1,000,000 will feel 1,000 times better! I will finally be truly happy! When I make a million dollars, my life will be fulfilled.*

Besides, what did I have to lose? I really had nothing else going for me and there weren't any other burning offers coming my way . . .

And so, I marked that X on my map. That day, I became a professional treasure hunter, hunting the treasure that I thought would bring me happiness.

I relentlessly attacked this new goal. All the time, effort, and energy I'd previously put into playing basketball, I now funneled into making one million dollars. Nothing was going to stop me. This was the surefire way to my endless happiness.

For the next five years of my life, I didn't have a permanent residence. If someone wanted to send me a letter, they had to mail it to my parents' house in Kansas City; somehow, someway, they would get it to me. If you wanted to track down where I was in the world, well, good luck. Your best bet was to hop on a Southwest Airlines or Air China flight; the likelihood I'd be sitting next to you was actually relatively high.

I spent many nights sleeping in my car en route to my next

camp, or sleeping sitting straight up in the hardest plastic airport chairs ever created with horribly loud pop music blaring (because international airports specifically discourage people from spending the night . . . but that didn't stop me). Hostels equaled a great night's sleep for me—and *couches?* Now, those were an absolute luxury!

I spent many nights in the houses of strangers, including one memorable couple in Cairns, Australia. The husband was a sharp knife butcher, and their home was decked out like a horror movie with unimaginably large knives and blades. I slept in the open air of Uganda, minus the essential malaria nets (yeah, probably not the best choice—young and naive). I spent sleepless nights driving hours upon hours deep into the Australian outback on the wrong side of the road under the watchful eye of hundreds of kangaroos, just to run a basketball camp for maybe twelve kids in a small country gym. I once spent a week popping any ancient Chinese medicine balls I could find, terribly ill from eating a skewer in Beijing's Tiananmen Square (a skewer that I discovered was actually undercooked rat meat covered in lamb urine so that it would taste like chicken—not a "delicacy" I wish on anyone). Even though I literally felt like I might die of food poisoning, I still forced myself to run five hours of basketball camps for five consecutive days.

I survived. But barely. I learned a lot of invaluable lessons and experienced a multitude of less-than-pleasant situations. It was reckless living. I wouldn't recommend this rolling stone lifestyle for everyone, but I was on my treasure hunt. Once I hit that X, once I got to that million dollars, that's when I could relax, take a year or two off and enjoy myself, and definitely slow my pace down. But only when I *made it.*

Five years of treasure hunting flew by; then, one morning, I woke up in a hostel in Australia to find an email from the Brooklyn Nets that changed the entire trajectory of my life. I was once again forced to scroll through my bank account. I needed to examine the progress I had made thus far towards my X.

Five years—so, I had $500,000 to my name, right?

Not even close. After all of the stress I'd put on myself, day in and day out, to hit that monetary X, I was a far cry from the halfway mark. Turns out it's not the money you *make*, it's the money you *save*. Somehow, I'd failed to factor in travel expenses, living expenses, taxes, insurance, or any other essential living costs into my brilliant million-dollar equation.

What I had saved during those five years were the life lessons learned. The experiences. Even though I hadn't always fully embraced the life adventure I was on, my personal growth far out-weighed the growth of my bank account. The thirty countries I traveled to, the relationships I formed knocking on doors and asking to run camps, sleeping in every condition under the sun—these things chiseled me each day, shaping me into the person I was becoming.

I'd been so singularly focused on getting to that X that I didn't realize how fun and amazing the actual journey was until it was already over. I didn't realize that my X could be worth far more than just a lump sum of money. I had valued physical treasure and what I'd thought it could provide for me as the *end goal.* But the real gold was in the daily experiences. Sure, it wasn't always the easiest (and it definitely wasn't always the most comfortable), but I wouldn't trade it for the world now—*not even for a million dollars.*

The kindness of my friend Kris and his wife showed me how to truly be *generous*. Staying on the large knife butcher's couch, I discovered how to have *trust*. Sleeping without a safety net in the dangerous Uganda air taught me *faith*. The hours I spent driving and flying all over the world displayed my own *determination*. On the days I fought for my life, I discovered I have an *unbreakable will*. I started out as coal, but walking through the intense fire of life, I became a diamond.

Treasure hunting is a tricky business. If, by chance, you are able to fend off the native island tribe that is constantly swinging machetes at your throat, avoid the quicksand looming around every corner, and survive on a diet of coconuts and crickets, you might finally reach that X. But what happens if you only find the skulls and bones of those who came before you? The *treasure box* might be empty; your reward would be empty.

None of my experiences are probably worth much to you personally. They shouldn't be—they aren't personal to you. But the same applies to tangible objects—money, the sports car everyone turns their head to look at, or that six-bedroom mansion on your Pinterest board. You can try to make a dollar bill feel personal to you, but guess what? You weren't the first to own that dollar bill, and you won't be the last. You can try to make a home and all its market value feel like it's completely yours, but a large market crash could occur, a wildfire could burn it down, an earthquake could shatter it, a hurricane could destroy it, and on and on. The ONLY treasures that you will, without a doubt, never have taken from you are your own personal life experiences, your own lessons learned, your own faith developed, and your own memories created.

If you place your X on something physical and tangible and you tell yourself you need to have that X, it'll drive you crazy. It'll steal your daily joy. It doesn't matter if the X on your map is a flat-screen TV, a new car, a mansion in the hills, or a million dollars—it is not going to solve all of your problems in life and it's not going to bring you happiness. In fact, you'll actually be setting yourself up to fail (and miserably) on a never-ending quest. You'll be chasing after a prize you will never win.

But there is a way to have our treasure, to have constant joy, riches beyond gold. The mindset that you need to pivot is understanding that *what we appreciate* actually *appreciates*. The value of our treasure, the things we consider most important in life, will continue to rise in our minds as we pursue it.

You can choose to have your treasure at any moment; it is where *you* put your X on the map. And only you make the choice. If you mark it with spending time with the ones you love, working a job you enjoy each day, helping your community, being grateful for the smallest of small gifts, and knowing that you have all you need right now, in this very moment, then you will be seeking a treasure worth much more than gold. And even better, this treasure continues to *grow*, along with your joy, your passion for life, your love for others, your contentment with who you are, and your confidence in yourself. Your anxieties and worries will diminish as you figure out exactly who YOU are, the unique treasures you have that no other single person can ever replicate.

Life is an adventure; enjoy it. Don't spend the next five years of your life missing the entire point (like I did in my quest for a million dollars), chasing some physical treasure chest you think will bring you happiness. It won't, I can promise you. That foggy afternoon in the Oakland Bay, I placed my X where I thought I wanted it to be. I just never realized that I had my X with me all along. The joy is in the journey.

BLUEPRINT ACTION PLAN

1. Directly above the largest X on the treasure map, write down where you want to be five years from now. Above each smaller x, write out five major steps that you'll have to take to get there.

Take a hard look at those steps—do they look like an amazing adventure?

Next to each, rank how excited you are about it on a 1-20 scale—1 being absolute misery, and 20 being absolute joy.

Add those five numbers together.

Now, out of 100%, you can foresee how much you'll enjoy life pursuing your X. Refill your map until you have 90% or higher! Don't settle for anything less than what you LOVE!

2. Write down "PLACE YOUR X WHERE YOUR JOY IS" on a notecard and put it in your wallet among your credit and debit cards. Each time you open your wallet to pay for something, take a moment to reflect on where you have placed your X.

WRITE OUT YOUR GOALS AND STEPS IN EACH OF THE BOXES

DAY 3
THE 18TH SECOND

REMEMBER THAT BOY WHO WAS twice as big as everyone else and already growing a mustache by the third grade? When I was growing up, that kid was Michael. (This isn't his actual name; I want to protect his privacy, for reasons that will soon be obvious.)

He came from a family that didn't have much money, and he struggled academically in school. But sports? That's where Michael thrived. He was vastly superior to everyone else our age athletically. A lot of it had to do with the fact that he was three feet taller than the rest of us, a height difference especially helpful in basketball. While I didn't have Michael's height advantage at the time, I was still one of the best kids on the basketball court, which is where we became friends.

As we got older and the rest of us got taller, Michael slowly began to fall behind the curve. Without that height advantage, he was left with the memory of once being the best basketball player—and the added pain of the unfulfilled expectations placed upon him by his family.

You see, his early athletic superiority had given his family the idea that, by way of basketball, he would be their ticket to a better life. That savior expectation would be daunting and burdensome for anyone, but it weighed even harder on Michael, who was still just a young kid.

This weight grew heavier and heavier as his basketball dominance wavered. His father had a solution, though: football. He told Michael, "You'll do great. All you got to do is be tough."

Now, just looking at the kid, you would understand why his father jumped to this plan. He was thick in stature and he gave off the impression that he was rugged and *tough*. However, his outward appearance belied his softer, more gentle countenance. On top of that, Michael didn't even *like* football.

I'm extremely grateful that I never had to carry the cross of expectations from my father. Nowadays, you can just Google "Andre Agassi" or "Todd Marinovich" for prime examples of how *not* to father a child. But even as a middle school kid, I could recognize that Michael was in a lot of emotional pain. It was obvious that the expectation he'd earn a college scholarship and play in the NFL weighed immeasurably on him. Some days when we were supposed to be relaxing and hanging out, he wouldn't say a single word to me because he was so engulfed with trying to please his father and the fear that he would never succeed.

However, Michael wound up being very successful on the high school football field and, surely enough, managed to get a college scholarship to play. During college, Michael and I didn't talk or check in on one another very much. We were both fully engaged in our "jobs," our respective college sport. As any college athlete can tell you, the intense time commitment makes it feel like a full-

PASSION

time job. Now, don't get me wrong, it's a GREAT job—but only if you absolutely love the sport you're playing.

Michael didn't. He didn't love football. He didn't love the daily grind of practice, or even the art of the sport itself. Most of all, he hated the physical pain that he had to endure every day. No matter how hard he tried, he couldn't find joy, excitement, or satisfaction in playing football. He just couldn't control his feelings.

However, Michael had to do *something* if he was going to survive (much less thrive) at football for the long haul. Which led to him forming a *mental dictatorship*.

Michael became a pain junkie. He learned that he could overcome physical pain with mental strength. The more physical pain he was put through while playing, the more strength he could show by overcoming it. Finally, for once in his life, he had the power to choose what he felt (or rather, what he wouldn't allow himself to feel). When he played, he shut off all natural instincts and forbid any feelings of vulnerability. He put his physical and emotional feelings aside so that he could train and play like he actually loved football and was willing to do anything to succeed at it. He chose to be in the weight room at five each morning, he ran hill sprints until his lungs bled, and he spent twice as much time watching football film as he did completing any school work. Without a single sniff from an NFL team, he decided he was going to train and play like he was already there. In his mind, the pain of not living up to his father's expectations far outweighed the pain he endured playing a sport he didn't enjoy.

After four years of this daily mental dictatorship, Michael, a former walk-on to a prominent Division 1 football powerhouse, was selected in the sixth round of the NFL draft. He had finally made it—an NFL tight end with a multi-million-dollar contract. He had arrived; he had achieved his goal. Well, he had achieved his father's goal. He had lived up to impossible expectations and succeeded.

Over the next seven years of his NFL career, Michael and I talked often, but when I'd ask if he was excited about the current season or the upcoming game or if he was loving life, his response was always the same—"Nope, not really. But it's what I do."

After Michael retired, I had lunch with him, his wife, and his newborn son in Phoenix. I was curious if he'd ever grown to love the game he'd dedicated all of his time and energy to for almost eighteen years (middle school through retirement). I wanted to know if he ever came to grips with the expectations that had been placed upon him by his father. Hoping that he'd had a mid-career awakening and realized he actually loved playing football and felt good about all he'd gone through, I asked him, "What have been the best days of your life?"

Now, of course, he began by talking about the day he got married and the day his son was born. But the part of his answer that stuck out the most, the part that made me queasy, was when he said "the day I retired from the NFL."

I don't condone the reason Michael developed his *mental dictatorship*. In fact, a secondary lesson we should take from this story is the relationship of purpose, passion, and pain. A person's purpose can be wasted pursuing a goal created for them selfishly by someone else. Be aware and wary of other's expectations of you: Do they align with what *you* want, or are they purely what *they* want? The same goes for the expectations you place on others: Always make sure your intentions are selfless.

Still, Michael taught me something valuable about *mental dictatorship*. When put towards a passion, it can change everything. If this guy, who *hated* football and didn't have the natural aptitude for it, was able to make an NFL career based off this brain-based superpower, what could that mean for someone who uses it to actually pursue something they love? So, I started exploring *mental dictatorship* for myself.

You know what I discovered?

Seventeen seconds. Literally, that's all it takes. After just seventeen seconds, you can impose your own mental dictatorship over nearly any task.

Now, there isn't an official study out there on this. I didn't take it down to a science lab. Instead, I studied myself.

I get a lot done in a day, and people are always asking me how; I never had a good answer until I did this study. I realized that I do a few things every morning to trigger my brain into creating my own *mental dictatorship*: I make my bed, I practice deep breathing (seven deep slow breaths, to be exact), and I take an ice-cold shower. These three simple staples massively influence how the rest of my day will go. Through trial and error, I've learned that they help me set up for the best day I can possibly have. The days that I start off with these three things are always much better than the days when I don't. It's just a simple fact. It sets me up to push through times when I don't necessarily feel like working. I know that I have the *mental dictatorship* power to trigger my body into doing things it doesn't want to always do.

Don't get me wrong: I love my life and the mission I am on. There are still times, even though I'm constantly pursuing my passion, that I don't necessarily *feel* like taking the necessary steps. Not everything is going to be roses and butterflies; creating the life you want can be a challenge. It can mean working an extra job to make side income to put towards the business you want to start. It can mean giving up some extracurricular activities or social events with friends so you can put in extra work towards your goal.

Personally, I don't wake up every morning enthusiastic about making my bed, sitting in silence while breathing deeply, or freezing my butt off in the shower. Trust me, I'm not a machine. I'm very human, and being very human means I pretty much never want to do any of these things.

But I know that once I start, I'm that much closer to finishing, and when I'm finished, I feel so much better about myself. It's the ignitor I need to kickstart my day.

I wondered how long it actually took to overthrow my mindset, to go from unenthused to pumped. So, I pulled out the iPhone stopwatch and timed myself for a month straight.

The number that kept popping up, over and over, was seventeen seconds. Seventeen seconds into the ice-cold shower and my body adapted to the freezing cold. Seventeen seconds of shifting my sheets around and I was already putting the pillows in their place. Seventeen seconds of deep breathing and I was relaxed, focused, and ready to attack my day. That was consistently the time at which my mind pivoted to *mental dictatorship.*

I started applying it to everything. Working out in the gym: when I didn't feel like working out at all, seventeen seconds after I started actively moving, I was ready to rock. Sitting down at the computer to write: after fighting through the first seventeen seconds, I was locked in and spilling my thoughts onto the screen. Cleaning the kitchen and bathroom: seventeen seconds in and I was off to the races, scrubbing like a man possessed.

That's the moment when my mind tells me, "We are good, we've overcome it, we can make it through, and we won't just *survive*, we can *thrive.*"

Now, it's time to ask yourself—in what ways can you implement seventeen seconds of *mental dictatorship?* To reach your goals, you must take the first step to begin. The first step can be the most difficult. But now you have the power and you have the knowledge.

Seventeen seconds is all it takes.

BLUEPRINT ACTION PLAN

1. On the stopwatches, write down three things that you are going to use to build your mental dictatorship—three things you're going to muscle through for seventeen seconds each, fifty-one seconds every day. Is it going to be an ice-cold shower? Starting that first push-up? Opening up the Word document? Whatever has seemed like drudgery in your past, break three tasks off that you can start in seventeen seconds, and commit to using them for twenty-nine days—not only will you build your mental dictatorship, it will become part of your lifestyle and take you closer to achieving your goals each day!

2. Write down "IT ONLY TAKES 17 SECONDS" on a notecard and tape it to your microwave. Each time you set that timer, take the opportunity to reflect on how quickly you're able to heat up your whole mindset!

DAY 4
COLD CALLS

How awesome are cold calls?

Well, not to make. That part is awful and absolutely terrifying. As humans, we fear rejection—any type of rejection. Even from a complete stranger, it rocks our self-confidence to the core. The idea of hearing "no" ninety-nine times makes most of us break out in a cold sweat. To be honest, we'd probably rather stand in front of a large crowd naked before we pick up the phone and dial to make a cold call.

But the reality is that cold calling is awesome—taking the risk is awesome—even the *rejection* is awesome! Why? Because it is a decisive action in pursuit of opportunity. Even if we rack up 9,999 "noes," they are all worth it to hear the one right "yes."

Many parts of my early basketball career were punctuated by some of the most painful "noes" I've ever experienced. All I wanted was to play in the NBA, which takes some height, and I never hit the 6'6" frame my childhood doctor literally promised me. Malpractice! When I realized 6'2" was the limit, I semi-abbreviated my dream—I just wanted to play professionally.

At twenty-four, my professional playing career ended abruptly, in Azpeitia, Spain. I left the season early—in all honesty, not by choice (like I told everyone), but because I was cut. I was not good enough. I wasn't good enough in the eyes of a second-division, middle-of-nowhere, Basque-region Spanish team. A team comprised of players who treated the game like a hobby, more interested in which nightclub they'd hit till four in the morning *after* the game than anything that actually happened on the court *during* the game.

Playing basketball was who I was, it's what I had lived and breathed my entire life, and that rejection ripped my entire identity away from me.

It literally haunted my dreams. I would wake up consistently in the middle of the night drenched in sweat. I felt extremely bad for myself. I didn't want to be around other people, not even my friends. (God forbid anyone ask me the most dreaded question: "What are you going to do now?") I rarely came out of my room. I felt like I had let everyone down. I'd put all my life marbles into basketball, and now they'd all rolled away.

A few weeks into this downward spiral, I was eating my favorite fruit and granola yogurt parfait for breakfast when my mom broke my depressed silence.

"David, you know, when one door closes, another door, window, and entire home open."

I was completely caught off-guard. Sure, I'd heard the saying that when one door closes another opens, but what was this about an entire home?

"What?" I responded.

"Yes, God has far greater things in store for you than you can imagine. Far greater than just another door. He's got an entire

FAILURE

home waiting," my mom said, continuing to put away the dishes without breaking her stride.

My mom's wisdom greatly impacted me that day, and it's stuck with me ever since. It helped me realize that I had to stop staring sadly back at that shut-and-locked door of my past and start looking around for the house on the market that was my future. I wasn't looking for another door—I was looking for a mansion. My dream mansion had always been the NBA; if I couldn't play in it, I needed to figure out another way in.

I knew it was time to take action.

The next morning, I woke up early, scarfed down my delicious parfait with much more vigor than I'd had the day before, and got straight to work. I looked up every phone number of every NBA GM. And I cold called *all of them.*

Not one answered. (For those of you keeping score, that's thirty implicit "noes.")

I left a message for each of them, but I wasn't going to let my fate be determined by waiting for calls back. I had to do something to stand out from everyone else trying to break into the NBA.

Email was too easy. I got back on the computer and I searched until I found every physical address of each team. I wrote, and I wrote, and I wrote until the fingers on my right hand literally went numb. I sent every GM a full-page, handwritten letter. I didn't ask for a job; I simply told them about myself and then I pointed out the unique features I liked about their franchises and the way they ran their teams.

I knew I wasn't going to get hired from my resume. Trust me, you're never going to get your dream job by sending a resume online and crossing your fingers some person who doesn't know you from Adam will hire you. It's ALL about relationships. Genuine, true relationships. People hire people they know, people they trust, people they want to be around. I wasn't cold calling (or cold letter-writing) to sell anything; I was extending my hand, introducing myself, and beginning the process of building those relationships. At the end of each letter, I wrote, "If there is anything I can do for you, anything at all, I would be more than happy to serve you and your organization." That's the key in building new relationships: give, give, give, and give some more, without ever expecting anything in return.

One NBA GM called me back. Of all the calls I made and the letters I wrote, one got back to me. I went 1 for 30. That is literally 3.3%. But that single "yes," that *one* opportunity, helped me unlock the doors to my dream mansion.

Gary Sacks, GM of the Los Angeles Clippers, returned my call. At the time, the Clippers were just beginning to get sexy as the up-and-coming franchise in the NBA; they had been the cellar-dwellers for many years, but Gary was helping turn the entire organization around. He was a big name in the NBA. (The following season, he would place second for the NBA Front Office Executive of the Year.)

Our conversation was short and concise; he asked me about myself and thanked me for the card I sent. He ended the call by giving me his personal email and saying, "If you are ever in LA, let me know. We'll get some coffee."

Boom. All I needed to hear. Most might have taken it as a polite "best of luck with the rest of your life." To me, it was my Willy Wonka golden ticket. The moment I hung up, I got on Southwest. com to find flights out of Kansas City.

"Mom, I'm going to LA next week," I yelled up the stairs.

Two days before my scheduled trip, I emailed Gary and told him I would be in town to run a basketball camp. (I wasn't really running a camp, but I didn't want him to think I was desperate. Hungry, yes, but not desperate. There is a very fine line between the two.) Not thirty minutes later, he emailed back, telling me to meet him at his office at the Clippers facility in Playa Vista, a beach suburb of LA.

I was in. The work I'd done to distinguish myself from others paid off. I went the extra mile (well, 1600 miles, to be exact) to meet Gary in person, and it began a genuine relationship. I actually ended up living with him and his family for a few months when I decided to move to LA years later. Today, I call Gary one of my best friends in the world. I talk with him nearly every other day and we frequently go on basketball-related trips together. He was a groomsman in my wedding and someone I lean on for guidance in any work decision I make. We have an awesome friendship. And it's all because of a cold call. I wound up finding a lifelong friend and an NBA connection who has proved extremely helpful in my journey, all because I wasn't too afraid to pick up the phone and possibly hear the dreaded word "no."

Most people spend the majority of their twenties going out after work with their friends to happy hours. They spend weekends bar-hopping, searching for a good time, chasing the here-and-now with the group of people they are comfortable around. The twenties are what I call the "extended college years" (though some of us extend them well into our thirties and beyond). You've got your college degree, you're still invincible, and "real-life" will begin whenever you want to hit the start button. But your friends are going out this evening and again this weekend, so . . .

I'm not saying anything against going out, having fun, and hanging with your friends; that's okay, as long as your priorities fall in line with your goals. If your goal is to rarely ever move up the ladder and be stuck in the nine-to-five clock-in, clock-out mode while simply going through the motions, then yes, you are right on track. However, if your goals are bigger than just settling into your present role, if you want more than to just fit in with the crowd, then extending those college years might not be the way to go. Actually, let me be brutally honest—it's absolutely NOT the way to go.

I spent my college years having too much fun; I was more interested in my social life than my educational one. I chose a major that I thought would be easy, rather than studying something I was actually passionate about. I didn't put in the effort to form a single relationship with any of my professors; popularity with my peers was more important to me. After years of caring more about which party I would go to or which bar would have the best girls, I graduated with a master's degree that I didn't have any interest in pursuing. I wasted five years that could have been very valuable.

Luckily, I chose to stop wasting years post college. Once I saw the effects of cold calling, I became addicted . . . not to happy hour-ing, but to developing genuine relationships. I learned to

FAILURE

love making new connections. I made it a fun game to talk my way into places that I didn't have any business being in, somehow fooling others into thinking that I more than belonged. At events, I challenged myself to collect as many business cards and talk to as many people as possible. This is probably where I developed a lot of the unwavering confidence I have in any situation. (However, word of wisdom: Never pretend to be something you're not. I realized I should steer clear of that charade early on, after I was caught in a group conversation with individuals I had each given a different story to. When they realized that I was apparently studying to become a rocket scientist, a Navy SEAL, *and* an open-heart surgeon, the conversation didn't end well. Makes for a funny story, but if you're gonna get up the nerve to talk to someone, make better use of it!)

I don't believe in "networking." Not in the way the world defines it, anyway. Networking, to me, is a dirty term that implies one person is using another to simply get ahead. I believe in forming genuine, reciprocal, and honest relationships. In fact, forming these relationships is more important than anything I could have studied in college (or at least anything that I did study . . . which wasn't much). Once I realized this, I started hopping on planes and following connections that were given to me by one person, which led to the next and then the next. By the time I was twenty-six, I had an enviable list of relationships with people ranging from NBA GMs to high-powered Silicon Valley venture capitalists to Wall Street investors. Instead of getting my highs from partying and stretching out the extended college years, I enjoyed knowing that

I was building something much bigger, forming relationships that would last a lifetime and eventually grow into my main support team. That work laid the foundation for the growing network of resources and friendships that are so important to me today. Now I've got someone in nearly every major country for nearly every situation you can think of that I can call on—not just a person, but a genuine friend. Give, give, give, and give some more, without ever expecting anything in return, and watch what blossoms in your life!

Whether you adopt this approach in your twenties or your fifties doesn't matter. It is never too late to become the driver of your own network. Let me emphasize: it's NEVER too late. Start today; pick up the phone and make a cold call or thirty. It only takes one yes.

FAILURE

BLUEPRINT ACTION PLAN

1. In the phones, write down five people you would like to get to know. (They can be in your field of work, in your life, even notoriously busy or famous people.) What interests you about them? What skillsets do you have that you'd like to offer to them? Search online for their phone numbers and give them a call. If you can only find email addresses and social media profiles, reach out and ask them for phone numbers. Don't get discouraged if you don't get anyone on the line at first—remember, I had a 3.3% success rate. Make a habit of calling five new people each week, and you will build AMAZING relationships. When you do connect with someone, ask what you can do to help them—give, give, give!

2. Write down "I CAN MAKE A COLD CALL" on a notecard and place it next to your phone charger. Commit to taking an inventory of how your cold call list for the week is coming along every time you plug in your phone.

DAY 5

$120,000 BELOW MOUNT EVEREST

TED WAS CLEARLY KILLING IT. He lavished his wonderful wife with elegant dinner dates. They had a healthy, beautiful baby, a new house and a new car. He had a ton of friends, he was popular at the office, he was the star of happy hour with his "boys," and he was the envy of everyone, particularly on the golf course.

None of this was by accident.

See, Ted wanted his co-workers to envy him; he wanted to be the talk of the town; he wanted to be liked by others; and he wanted, more than anything, to be "the man" at the office.

Since all of this was based on comparison and competition with the people around him, Ted always had to stay on top, always had to do more to promote his image. When a co-worker got a new car, Ted upgraded his seven-month-old ride for a brand-new car that would really stand out and compete. He always picked up the tab for his buddies at happy hour or dinner, and he definitely made sure no one had nicer golf clubs. Ted was the master of what I call *the one-upness.* So much so that he was willing to spend money he didn't have just to keep up his image and lifestyle.

That's what credit cards are for though, right?

Deep down, Ted *knew* what he was doing; he knew his reckless spending was going to catch up with him at some point. He knew

. . . but he hadn't felt the pain of the consequences. In reality, Ted knew he needed to rein in his spending, pay his bills, and then work towards saving. But *knowing* and *doing* existed in two completely different dictionaries in Ted's mind-library.

The disconnect between *knowing* and *doing* runs much deeper than just the lethal comparison games. The majority of us know that we shouldn't eat half of the gooey chocolate cake in the fridge right before going to bed. It's no secret that sleep and exercise are important, but how many of us actually work these into our lifestyle habits? We know choosing to watch four hours of Netflix alone in the evenings, when we could be playing catch with our kids or helping them with their flute lessons instead, isn't the best way to create a strong family unit. But *knowing* and *doing* are completely different.

The same goes for comparison. We all *know* how detrimental comparison can be. We all *know* that comparing ourselves to other people will steal our joy and leave us feeling unworthy. Even if we compare ourselves to someone we see as "less than," that victorious feeling doesn't benefit us for much longer than a minute or two. Why? Because it will be just as easy to feel "less than" a different person in the same field. There will always be someone who is a little bit better, a little more experienced, a little more successful, and a little more (fill in the blank) than you. Comparison can provide a quick endorphin rush, but this high is very temporary. It's a high that people like Ted become addicted to and continually chase.

How many articles and podcasts have told you to stop comparing yourself, giving some sexy analogy that seems momentarily life-changing? Countless.

But there's a very big difference in *knowing* versus actually *doing*, isn't there?

So, today, I want you to forget what you *know*. I encourage you to compare yourself with *everyone* and *everything* around you. Don't be objective! Compare yourself to your ultimate go-getter co-worker. Compare yourself to the classmate from high school who gets five times as many likes on their social media posts. Compare yourself to every woman who appears on a magazine cover with flawless skin and a waistline that hasn't grown since elementary school. Compare yourself to the personal trainer with bulging biceps and an eternal-summer tan lifting weights next to you at the gym. Compare, compare, and compare some more. You know the neighbors who just went on that extravagant island getaway and still have the money to buy a hot tub the size of a small pool? And your child's classmate who is getting straight A's while learning two new languages on the side? And the person you heard about on the news who went from absolutely nothing to worth millions in a matter of weeks? Those are exactly the people you want to compare yourself to. Constantly. Don't stop! Don't take a break. For whatever portion you're awake of the next twenty-four hours, tear bits and pieces away from your whole self and hold them up in stark comparison with the best bits and pieces of anyone else that you can find. Nothing is too ridiculous. Hey look, that guy at the grocery store has ingredients you've never even heard of in his cart. Your neighbor's dog can hear the mailman before your dog can. Compare to no end!

Now, you're probably wondering, "How in the world is this

good advice?" It all seems contradictory and awful, right? You *know* comparison is pointless. You *know* that it will steal every ounce of your daily joy, chew it up, and spit it right back in your face. Yet . . . you've never *done* away with it.

So, when I tell you to compare yourself to everyone and everything you can for the next twenty-four hours, that's not anything different from what you usually do. I'm just telling you to do *more* of it! I want you to do an almost comical amount of it. The most you've ever done in one day, without hesitation or pause. Jump from one comparison to the next so quickly that you barely even leave time to heal from the blows. The goal? You will drive yourself nuts. Absolutely nuts. You will truly feel how useless and shallow the pain of comparison is. You will finally be ready to *do*—or, in this case, to *stop doing*.

Because you know what happens if you don't turn that *knowing* into *doing*? Do you know what happens if you let your comparisons shape the way you view yourself and dictate your daily actions?

It will eventually all come crashing down on you. Like the great Roman cities of the past, you will crumble to pieces.

Ted's life crumbled with a letter in the mailbox: "You have been evicted. You have five days to get all of your stuff out of the house. The property now belongs to the city."

That's right—the house was gone. And Ted's wife didn't even know they were in debt. Over $120,000 in credit card debt alone, actually. A Mt. Everest-sized avalanche of comparison had finally tumbled onto Ted's seemingly perfect life.

When Ted broke the news to his wife that evening at dinner, he choked back tears and tried to act like he had it all under control. His wife was forced to cycle through the stages of shock, anger, disappointment, and fear in less than two hours. Luckily, she didn't leave him; she agreed to handle the situation as a team this time. They *knew* they had to *do* something . . .

And they *did*. Ted finally *did*.

They moved themselves and their newborn into a two-bedroom, one-bathroom house with Ted's parents. There were no more happy hours, no more golf clubs, and no more elegant dinners. The envy and opinions that Ted had spent so much money trying to buy instantly evaporated, of course. His pride was tarnished. His reputation at the office took a huge Rocky Balboa right-hook to the jaw.

Ted swallowed his pride and slowly learned how to pivot from the constant need for comparison. He now fully realized the harsh reality of being a "one-upper." And it freed him and his family. They were able to pay off the $120,000 debt over the course of four years by staying consistent with their new habits and paying attention to their own needs and responsibilities. They executed a plan, they stuck together, and most of all, they refused to compare themselves to anyone around them. They were finally *doing* rather than just *knowing*.

And that's the drastic difference: do you *do* what you *know*, or do you get caught up in the joy-thievery of the comparison game? It's a game we all play at some point, but do you control it . . . or does it control you?

BLUEPRINT ACTION PLAN

1. Beside the vampire teeth, write down three points of comparison you regularly turn to over the course of your day. Be honest!

   Now, write down something that you admire and you're proud of in someone that you love. Make a commitment to pivot to these admirable thoughts each time you find yourself falling into particularly unhealthy comparison traps—you'll be amazed how quickly you can train your brain!

2. Write down "DOING VS. KNOWING" on a notecard and place it next to your computer either at the office or at home. Commit to reflecting on the nature of comparison any time you check social media and remind yourself that those likes and smiles never tell the whole story.

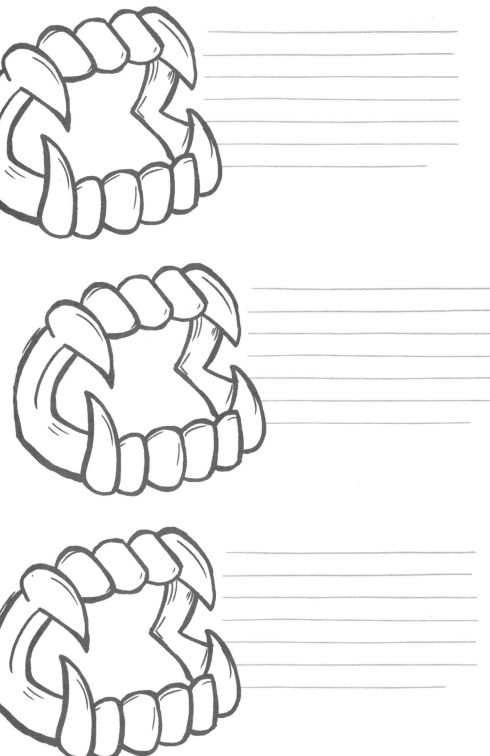

DAY 6
HARLEM GLOBETROTTERS, SWEDISH MEATBALLS, & GREAT WHITE SHARK DIVING

I HAD A DAY OFF from running basketball coaching clinics in Stockholm, so I went on the hunt for the finest, most gourmet Swedish meatballs. I mean, what else would you do with free time in Sweden, right? It was already late afternoon and the sun was just starting to set on the cobblestone streets of old-town when I finally decided on a spot. (The size of the meatballs sold me, along with the extra cheese on top.)

As I shoveled in my fourth massive meatball, I overheard a guy talking about scaling Everest. Obviously, this caught my ear. Then I heard him going on about diving with great white sharks . . . without a cage. Ok, now he *definitely* had my full attention.

After his next story, which involved chasing gorillas through the deep jungles of Uganda, I just had to jump in and find out if this guy was full of it. I asked him rapid fire questions, expecting to catch him in a lie. But instead, I realized the man was legit. Super legit.

As fate would have it, he was actually an adventure coach (a profession I'd never even knew existed, but immediately envied). This living, breathing Dos Equis Most Interesting Man in the World told me, "David, without adventure, you can't fully be alive. And without fully living, you will never stay young. To avoid challenge and fear and discomfort is basically synonymous with growing old and dying an early death."

That might seem a little extreme, but anything less than extreme advice from this mystery man would have been bizarre. We ended up talking for nearly two hours, and about fifteen massive meatballs later, I was inspired and hungry for something else: adventure and challenge.

I decided I would challenge myself four times a year—but not just four ordinary challenges. They needed to throw me out of my comfort zone and make me ask, "Am I alive, or just going through the motions?"

I embarked on a lot of adventures after that day in Sweden; I could probably talk your ear off with stories. Like the time I went diving with great white sharks off the coast of Australia, being scoped out as an appetizer by ocean beasts who, back in the pre-historic days, probably gave the dinosaurs a run for their money. Or the time I went skydiving over the Pacific Ocean, praying the guy attached to my back wasn't lying about having done this a time or two or a hundred before. (Great thought as you're free-falling 15,000 feet, right?) Or when I jumped off 100-foot cliffs on the island of Boracay in the Philippines. I love adventure (almost too much at times, according to my wife).

Attacking these types of challenges head-on makes me feel so alive. It makes me grow and understand my capabilities better. These moments are important in my life, and I believe they are just as important for you to have, too. The only catch? Unless you're an adventure coach, it's not realistic to include piranha feeding,

SUCCESS

Formula One race car driving, or African safari-ing into your daily routine. In reality, 99% of life is spent in the everyday grind; that "day after day after day" of doing the same thing. It's the ultimate Groundhog's Day: getting up in the morning when you would rather sleep in, going to a job you might not be overly excited by, driving back home through traffic to find your mailbox full of bills, sitting at the dinner table with your family, having "how-was-your-day" conversations on autopilot, and then thinking of all the things you have to do the next day as you climb into bed, worn out. Which is why, instead of focusing on crazy, adrenaline-pumping adventures like my encounters with sharks, skydiving, or cliff-diving, today, I'd like to tell you about the Harlem Globetrotters.

Whether you are a basketball fan or not, you've probably heard of the fun-loving Harlem Globetrotters. Known for bringing families together through their comedic tricks, goofy stunts, and upbeat energy, they make the game of basketball come to life like a Broadway play. Chances are, you're probably smiling right now, just thinking about them.

But have you ever really paid attention to the players on the opposing team?

Of course you haven't. No one has. The Washington Generals (the team that the Harlem Globetrotters "compete" against in this theatrical production) lose *every single game*. Every game. They do the same exact routine with the same exact choreographed moves, night after night, with no possible chance of winning. They have to play basketball like robots, acting out an already-scripted game that makes them the butt of every joke. But it's all in the name of family fun, right?

Well, up until now, less than a handful of people have known about one of my deepest secrets and darkest times, but it's finally time to come clean to the world: I was once one of those Generals.

Lace yourself up in my shoes; imagine the thing you love to do most in life. Your true passion. Whether it is painting, playing the guitar, being a great friend, or something else, it must be something deeply important that you take very seriously. Something you have poured lots of your time and energy into.

Now, take that thing and flip it completely on its head. Sit on all of the talent and progress you've earned, and do it poorly instead in front of a huge audience. Make a mockery of it, so they laugh hysterically at how bad you are.

For example, let's say your passion is for fine art, and you've dedicated years of your life to becoming an exceptional painter. You've given everything to make your passion into your life's work, to have an audience, and to gain a following. You finally get the opportunity—except, instead of using your God-given gift, you are forced to finger-paint stick figures that thousands of people will point and laugh at. You are featured in a famous gallery with another painter who is equally as talented as you, but in order to make that other painter look like the star of the show, you must produce only horrible art.

Inside, you are screaming, aching to tell gallery visitors that you have the ability to paint a masterpiece that will blow their minds. You desperately want to paint something truly beautiful.

But you and your finger-painting get invited to go on tour; seeing the world will make up for the terrible daily monotony and depressing waste of your talent, right?

Not exactly. You're shuttled directly in and out of arenas in all the amazing cities. You don't get to tour the town; you never actually even get to see the sun. You're locked in the concrete prison of the arena. You share a bus with a group of people you know for a fact you're more talented than—yet they are celebrated, they get to paint the masterpieces, and they are the ones that get the accolades, the praise, and the preferential treatment.

This doesn't just happen a few times. This is what every single day of your life looks like.

And that's exactly what playing for the Washington Generals was like for me.

I was recruited to the Generals right after I was released from the NBA D-League (literally the league one step below the best league in the world). How many other people have gone from nearly-the-NBA to the bottom-of-the-barrel Washington Generals, you might ask? NO ONE! So, to say my ego was hurt would be the understatement of a lifetime. But they sold me on the promise that I would still be able to follow my dream of playing high-level basketball every night while traveling to great cities throughout the world, all in preparation for a professional basketball career overseas. Little did I know that this would end up being much more like the high school musical that everyone was embarrassed to be in than it was actually a basketball game.

During the half time of a game in the "beautiful" city of Dayton, Ohio, I came into the locker room after my main part, which was defending a Globetrotter—chasing him around the court, falling down, getting my shorts pulled down, and, to top it off, having a bucket of shredded up paper (the water bucket joke) poured on my head. This was the twenty-first day of this in a row (though not the twenty-first time—it happened twice a day on the weekends).

I couldn't take it anymore. I couldn't go through another half of the game I loved being tarnished and thrown in my face. That's when I decided I was going to beat the Globetrotters.

Now, the Globetrotters never lost. Literally, never lost. A streak that had lasted twenty-four years—8,829 games in a row, to be exact. But I was going to end that. I'd had enough.

The rules are slightly different in these basketball games; there just so happens to be a four-pointer (a very deep three, closer to half court than the actual three-point line). It was always scripted for the game to be somewhat close in the fourth quarter, which amped up the manufactured drama when the 'Trotters "miraculously" pulled away, making a mockery of us Generals. But not tonight! My master plan was to get hot from the four-point line late in the game instead.

There was 6:49 on the clock when I checked into the game in the fourth quarter. (That number is burnt in my brain, trust me.) I knew I would have to bide my time before I started going off script, and I prayed like crazy that I got hot that night.

And I did.

Bam, first four-pointer, nothing but net. Generals within three points. Next time down, another four-pointer. Generals now up one. I remember looking over at the Globetrotters coach; with a puzzled look on his face, he mouthed the words, "What the hell are you doing?" The Globetrotters scored the next time down on a set-up, beyond-choreographed play to take the one-point lead.

Timeout called. 2:56 to go in the game. The 'Trotters assistant came over to our huddle and said, "Take it easy, play the script out. This is how we make our money; you know there's no damn chance you're winning this game."

Too bad—I *was* winning this game.

Back on the court, I chose my four-point opportunities carefully, knowing that if I shot too much, they would take me out of the game in fear that I would actually beat the Globetrotters. (To be honest, I'm kind of amazed that they kept me in at all, since it seemed like I'd gone rogue—which I had.)

Down two with just over a minute left, the score was far closer this late in the game than we'd ever been. The game-ending play was set up; I was supposed to catch the ball and act like I was going to make a cool crossover move, allowing my defender to steal it, sprint to the other end, and throw the ball off the backboard for an alley-oop. This would be followed, as it had always been, by "Sweet Georgia Brown" (a song that still gives me nightmares) and an extended dance on court where even the crowd joined the celebration.

Too bad; today, I had different plans.

As I went to crossover, instead of putting the ball out in front of me so my 'Trotter defender could get it, I quickly pulled it back closer to my body. He completely whiffed, getting all air and stumbling out of the picture. Now, wide open on the four-point circle, I let it fly—literally a slow-motion, made-for-movies shot. It hit the front of the rim . . . and rolled in! One-point lead for the Generals.

Everyone on the court was in shock. The Globetrotters were

cursing at me as I ran back down the court, and my teammates on the Generals really had no idea how to react, other than to stay cemented and keep doing exactly what they always do.

Timeout called with 39 seconds left in the game.

I got pulled. I got chewed out relentlessly. 'Trotters ended up winning the game, of course. And I quit the next day.

I'm not saying quitting is the solution to a problem or a difficult situation. I believe we develop a lot of toughness and grit by sticking something out we might not want to.

But when it's our lives, when it's the loss of another precious day to something we don't want to give our precious days to, then it isn't about developing toughness and grit—it's about not wasting time just because we feel obligated. We don't have to put up with an endless string of days that kill our passion, our joy, and our lives. We can choose our own journey—we can choose our own adventure. That is our superpower, *choice*. And you can use that superpower every single day. It's not a one-time use thing. Sure, we will face monotonous days, weeks, maybe even months that feel like we're trying to run a marathon in quicksand, but they are only worth it if they are actually part of a bigger picture, a bigger adventure. If you're not excited about the mission you are on, if you don't find any pleasure in the outcome you're anticipating, then it's time to flip the script. It's time to make an adventure and free yourself up for a mission that you're passionate about.

Life is an adventure—enjoy it. There's no excuse to grind it out and go through life on autopilot; if you're miserable with what you're doing and there's no end in sight, *go rogue*. We are not robots; we are superheroes with the superhero power of CHOICE!

SUCCESS

BLUEPRINT ACTION PLAN

1. In the arrows , write down three things in your daily life that feel like an absolute grind, but are necessary to your mission.

Now, inside the stars, write out three adventures you want to go on completely outside your comfort zone. Think big picture adventures on these, not daily adventures (unless you are an adventure coach yourself!).

Now, inside the circles, find the ways that you can use your grind tasks to contribute to your adventure goals! For example, let's say I hate cleaning the kitchen and I want to climb Everest—by cleaning the whole kitchen while doing an extra set of mountain climbers, I get my body a tiny bit more ready for a big climb. One of my next adventures is going to be running a basketball camp in Antarctica. The way I'm preparing for it? Visualizing shooting a basketball while taking a three-minute ice cold shower. Not only am I getting in gear for the frigid adventure itself, I'm getting the endorphin rush of prepping every single day!

2. Write down "LIFE IS AN ADVENTURE, ENJOY IT" on a notecard and place it next to where you keep your shoes. Commit to repeating the phrase aloud and preparing yourself to attack another day of adventure and joy as you put on your shoes each morning.

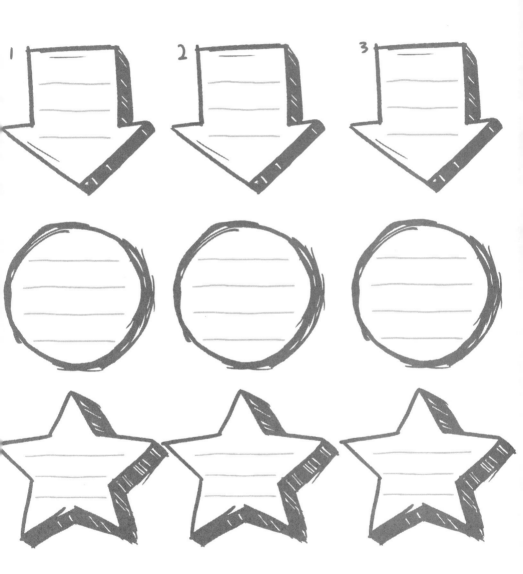

DAY 7

HIGH STAKES POKER & SUSHI IN CLEVELAND

I BECAME CLOSE FRIENDS WITH a very young, very impressionable NBA player when I was coaching for the Brooklyn Nets. We'll call him Marcus for the sake of the story. (Sorry, can't give you his real name!)

Marcus was a great kid—kindhearted, not extravagant, and a loving, committed boyfriend to his high school sweetheart. But Marcus was a follower.

High-stakes poker games are common on NBA flights. And I mean *really* high stakes. I've seen over $20,000 change owners in one hand. These games are normally reserved for the older, more well-off vets, but occasionally a young buck will muscle his way in. This time, it was Marcus. He was just beginning his NBA career, so he wasn't making the type of money the veterans around him were (especially the All-Stars). But between the peer pressure and his desire to fit in, Marcus couldn't let anyone think he wasn't able to live the lifestyle.

The bad news? Marcus didn't even know how to play poker. I'll let you imagine how those games went.

Have you heard the ridiculous stories about the "groupies" who line up at the hotels and wait for NBA players and coaches to return after the game? Well, they're true. All of them. I remember being accosted by chirps while walking back to the hotel at LA Live after getting beat by the Lakers; four less-than-modestly dressed girls asked me if I knew Marcus. They were all there for him.

The pressure to fit in consumed him, and Marcus visibly fell victim to his environment. Soon, he was covered in tattoos, wearing gold chains far more expensive than he could afford, losing entire paychecks every poker game, and scoring more with random women than on the court. Marcus was lost.

I saw this unfold like a slow-motion car crash, and I knew I had to do something about it before he ended up out of the league and broke. I truly believe that one of the worst things you can do to a person is *not* try to help them up when they fall, so Marcus' downward spiral landed him in a very scary place—a sushi restaurant in Cleveland.

Don't ask me why I picked sushi. One of my core principles is to never eat sushi more than 100 miles from the ocean, and Cleveland might be the furthest city in America from the ocean. But regardless, I took Marcus to this restaurant, and as they delivered the hand rolls, I started asking him questions.

"Where do you want to be in five years?"

"An NBA All-Star on a max contract."

"And what are you doing every day to get a step closer to that goal?"

"Hoop."

(In basketball lingo, the term "hoop" means to dominate on court—basically be "the man" in the games.)

FAILURE

"Marcus, you're not even getting minutes on the floor, my man."

I asked if he thought the life he was living aligned with his goals. I asked him about his girlfriend. I asked him about his finances. I asked him if he could look at himself in the mirror and be proud of the person staring back.

That's when he broke, and a tsunami of guilt, burdens, pressures, fears, and inadequacies came crashing down. Between the vices I'd already known about, hard drugs and alcohol binges, Marcus had reached bottom.

Past midnight and at least twelve sub-par sushi rolls later, Marcus and I had devised a game plan. He would take control of his environment. He would not let his surroundings, teammates, and the peer pressure of fitting in derail his life and steal his identity.

Marcus changed that night—not all at once, but in small, incremental steps. He had a game plan. Marcus had recognized he wasn't being true to who he really was, and he became the master of his own choices. His NBA career is now healthy, his relationship with his high-school sweetheart is healthy, and he is healthy. He takes young teammates under his wing and mentors them on the importance of avoiding the peer pressure of "living the life" in the NBA. He hasn't reached his goal of becoming an NBA All-Star yet. But then again, it hasn't even been five years.

Do you ever wonder why the vastly overweight receptionist with six "client" candy bowls spread across her desk can't seem to lose weight? Or why the father with a mobile office in the kitchen and a small desk in the family room can never shut off his work?

Ever seen a biker gang walk into a restaurant, or a group of college frat boys hanging at the mall? Whether we want to admit it or not, our choices and our actions are shaped by our environments and the people we surround ourselves with.

You've probably heard "You are the sum of the five people you spend the most time with." It's true. Part of human nature is yearning to find our "community." Don't get me wrong—community is great! We all need community; we can't do life on our own and we need support systems around us. However, the people in your community shape you. We get to customize and choose the people we spend the most time with like toppings at our favorite ice cream shop. If we choose to make ourselves sardine and garbage sundaes, we're probably going to smell like trash.

Without even realizing it, our environment shapes who we are. It determines what habits we develop, and our habits define us. Think about this: If I'm trying to avoid late night eating so that I get better sleep, and I have a stash of Doritos laying out in my bedroom that I have to pass before crawling into bed, am I likely to take a handful? Probably. It would be ideal to just not have a bag of Doritos in my house to begin with, but let's be realistic. We all have an unhealthy treat or two stashed somewhere, right? So, let's say I put the bag in the cabinet furthest away from my bedside and I put a child lock on it. Making the chips into a chore changes my behavior to help me reach my goals. And it's all just based on the way I've set up my own environment.

Set up your environment the way you want your best day to be set up. Personally, I surround myself with the things I know are

FAILURE

going to help me grow into the person I want to become. I keep my Bible, my guitar, pictures of family and loved ones, and my calendar of daily events nearby. There's a kettlebell by my door to ensure I pick it up and give it a few swings before I walk out. I have a standing desk for my computer, so I stand and type efficiently rather than browse the web aimlessly. I keep large water jugs right next to my workstation to make sure I'm always hydrated. These things help me live the best day that I possibly can every day, all facilitated by the environment that I have created.

Take on this challenge right now (as there is never a better time than *today*): Shift two or three things in your room/house that you know you shouldn't really have in easy proximity and replace them with things that will help you continue to grow into the person you want to become. It's a small mindset pivot, but one that can make all the difference in your day and your life.

BLUEPRINT ACTION PLAN

1. See that good lookin' stick figure? That's you!

Unfortunately, there are toxic and unstable elements in your environment. We all face them; the difference between leading the life you want and leading a life controlled by them is the good things we put between ourselves and those nasty things.

Beside the thorn, write down something toxic that you've been struggling with, something that truly hurts and poisons your daily life. Beside the rock, write down something destabilizing—something that throws your days into chaos.

Now, beside the flowers, write down the good aspects of your environment you have or can build to protect and distance you from the thorn and the rock. Whether those flowers are changes in your environment or stronger relationships with good people, take note— these are the things you need to nurture and draw closer to you!

2. Write down "I AM MY ENVIRONMENT & WHO I SURROUND MYSELF WITH" on a notecard and tape it to a flowerpot with a healthy plant in your home. Take a few minutes each day to care for this plant and reflect on the people and things in your life that help you grow and thrive.

DAY 8

RUSSIAN 'KUNG-FU' MASTER LOST IN THE STREETS OF BRAZIL

THE MAN WHO HIRED ME to work for the Brooklyn Nets was the owner and multi-billionaire Russian tycoon, Mikhail Prokhorov. Hardly anyone at the organization had personally interacted with Mikhail, so I didn't think much of the fact that I'd never met or even seen the guy before I got the job. Like an international man of mystery, he was rarely in the United States. But of course, as fate would have it, I'd been on court with the team for less than a week when I got the summons. Mikhail wanted to meet with me. Privately. Uh oh.

Now, I'm pretty well-versed at expressing my thoughts and theories on how to best work with NBA players and get the most out of their talent. But in the face of this imminent meeting, my mind went into overdrive worrying about the unknown and the million different ways it could play out.

I literally ran every single scenario in my head that you can think of—shoot, I even considered the possibility that my answers would be so bad that I would not only be fired, but banned from the NBA and sentenced to live out the rest of my life in a Russian prison.

Yeah, I was worried.

I arrived at the Ritz-Carlton in downtown Manhattan around eight in the morning, and I was immediately escorted to a secret elevator that took me to the top floor. This entire floor was the private penthouse of Mr. Prokhorov. One he owned, but rarely ever inhabited. (Let me tell you, if I lived in this penthouse, the idea of going anywhere else would not even enter my mind!)

I was told to wait on the couch in his library until he was ready. Going over my notes with butterflies racing to my throat, I waited for at least an hour, but it seemed more like four.

Mikhail walked into the room, and all 6'8" of him loomed over me. He stared into my eyes without saying a word. Now I started to worry that I hadn't worried *enough*!

Finally, he broke the silence in a thick Russian accent: "I've been training for four hours this morning."

I gulped and searched for the right words, settling eventually on a confused but faintly encouraging, "Great."

Immediately, he reached for me. "Now, we train."

Oh man, what am I in for? I wasn't worried anymore about impressing him with my insight on shooting or proving I could develop his NBA team. Making it out of here alive would be a victory in itself.

We walked into another room (one of many in his penthouse); it was all set up with yoga mats, medicine balls, tennis balls, a massage table, and some tools that looked like they should be on a surgeon's table instead of in a workout room.

So, there we were, just me and Prokhorov, in a room so secluded and secret that if anything happened, not a single soul would know (a thought that crossed my mind multiple times over the next two hours).

See, Prokhorov is not a man of ordinary interests. His passion is for Tescao Tibetan Martial Arts, a very rarely practiced form based on core balance, flexibility, and hand-eye coordination. It's meant to increase concentration, determination, and serenity all at once. Great skills to have, but packaging them all together is a little overwhelming, as I, his guinea pig, can attest to.

Prokhorov put me through exercise after exercise. There was an occasional move or two that I would immediately complete and conquer, but for the most part, I had to fail badly, many, many times, literally falling on my face before Mikhail decided we'd move on to the next. Every time I failed, Mikhail laughed at me and demonstrated it correctly. But as long as I got to move on, still alive, I was perfectly fine with that.

Which brings me to the *real application* of Tescao: Mikhail was going to show me what his Russian people used it for.

"Strike me," he said, accent heavy as ever.

Come again? I thought.

"Strike me," he repeated.

I slowly and methodically went in for a soft, across-the-body punch, aiming to land on his chest.

Like flash of lighting, he grabbed my arm and put me into something that resembled a 'death hold'—if that's a thing that exists outside '70s kung-fu movies.

"I could kill you right now," he growled into my ear.

Completely frozen, I didn't utter a word.

A few seconds passed like hours, and with a deep-chested, hard laugh, he let me go and smacked me on the back. "I'm only kidding."

I couldn't find any words, so I just smiled and quickly thanked God that my neck wasn't snapped in half.

Then, with a pat on my back and a "Good job, I like you," Mikhail decided to hit the showers before his next meeting.

I asked him for his phone number or email, acting like I would be practicing Tescao daily and wanted to let him know how well my training came along. Really, I just wanted to be a part of his 'inner circle'—after all, never hurts to have one of the most powerful people in the world on your side.

Instead of his personal info, I got exactly what I should have expected—a deep stare into my soul, and a firm, "When I am in town, you will know." He had no cell phone; he had no email. He had people to take care of stuff like that for him. (Probably the same people that he would now have watching me from the shadows.)

Too bad I didn't have Prokhorov's people watching over me when I ended up stranded all alone somewhere south of Recife, Brazil. To this day, I don't even know the exact name of the place; all I know is that it took two hours to get there, driving through one poverty-stricken favela after another. Eventually, I landed in a city that was actually quite large and appeared to have fairly decent infrastructure and an upbeat vibe. (Though most places in Brazil have an upbeat vibe—think Carnival.)

I was there to put on a basketball clinic and play in a game with the locals that everyone would come out to enjoy. Before I got started, the two people that had been kind enough to drive me down took me to lunch with their local friend. I spent the meal half marveling, half overwhelmed at the Portuguese language spoken about a million miles per hour. Their friend didn't know or understand a single word of English; on my best days, I can muster out the occasional thank you (*obrigado*).

The day flew by as fast as the Portuguese was spoken, and by the end of the clinic and the game, I was famished. The kids of the coaches and spectators wanted to play a game of their own, so I was off the hook. Time to feast!

When I'm traveling, I absolutely LOVE indulging in whatever foods the local people eat. If I'm in Israel, that's hummus with every meal; if I'm in Japan, I'm eating my favorite locally baked Japanese sweet potatoes and sushi. Here in Brazil, I was on a mission to find some fresh authentic açai.

My friends had kids playing in the youth game, but a coach I had just met offered to have his driver take me to get açai. Absolute no brainer: I was all in!

"I'll be right around the corner!" I yelled to my friends as I walked out the door, totally in control of the situation.

However, the driver had different plans. We drove for at least twenty minutes, taking turn after turn; there was a better chance of me learning the entire Portuguese language that night than finding my own way back to my friends.

After the Dr. Seuss-esque journey, we finally pulled up at an açai stand. I told the driver (who also spoke zero English) to wait right there; I would be back in a minute.

Surely enough, as soon as I stepped out of the car . . . he drove off.

"Ok, not a big deal," I thought, "he's probably just going to find a parking spot so he can join me for one of Brazil's special gifts to the world, a giant açai bowl with bananas and honey on top. Heaven in a bowl!"

Five minutes went by as I enjoyed the first bite; then ten. After fifteen, I'd licked the bowl clean, but my driver was still nowhere to be found.

"Did he park around the corner? Is he in the grocery store down the street? Maybe he had to pick up some milk and eggs for the family."

Trying to remain calm, I walked into the grocery store and asked everyone in sight if they spoke English, looking around for my driver. No response, no driver.

Another twenty minutes went by as I waited nervously on the street corner. Nothing.

I walked back to the açai stand to ask if anyone spoke English, only to be greeted with laughs and shoulder shrugs.

Forty-five minutes went by. An hour. It was over; I was lost in Brazil. It was time to pack it in and look into local real estate, because there was no chance anyone was going to find me. My mind raced; I wondered what my parents were going to think. What would my friends think? Would everyone write me off as dead? Maybe I could start walking north, hoping to eventually hit Recife, or just keep walking all the way up Central America, through Mexico and into Texas. It was possible. But probably not likely. And yet, even without a compass, that was probably my best shot. (You have to remember, this was before cell phones were attached to our hips, before widespread international phone service and Wi-Fi. Before Uber. Especially in middle-of-nowhere Brazil.)

I was young in my faith in Christ, and didn't really know if I actually believed in miracles. I loved the way living for God made me feel, the joy it brought me, but could prayers really be answered on the spot? I was very skeptical. But what did I have to lose?

I sat down on the curb and said aloud, "God, I need you on this one. It's just me and you. I'm lost, and without you, I'm never going to see my family again. Please help me."

Crickets. No response back from God; nothing changed. I put my face in my hands and began to cry.

Then I heard a horn honk.

I didn't move.

I heard it honk again. Whatever, I wasn't going to interrupt a good cry for traffic.

Finally, after the third honk, I looked up and saw the man I'd met at lunch earlier in the day.

Why was he even looking for me? How on earth did he know where to find me? I never told him where I was going, I never even told him I was leaving the gym, and it's not like he would have understood me if I had: he spoke absolutely zero English. Come to think of it, I don't think he was even at the gym after our lunch. But there he sat in his car, waiting for me to hop in.

I popped up off the curb faster than Usain Bolt, opened the door, got in, and threw my arms around this *angel* stranger.

"Thank you, thank you, thank you," I said, over and over again. Thank you, random Brazilian *angel*, and thank you God!

We are not in control, no matter how much we try or believe we can be. The desire to feel in control is one of extreme discontent and uneasiness. Understanding there is something bigger that has control over you, your circumstances, and your life plan can be the most freeing realization you will ever have.

I didn't die. I didn't get fired. I didn't get sent away to a Russian prison for life. I didn't have to live out my days in Brazil. Instead, I gained memories that I will never forget and a trust and faith that far transcend any feeling of complete control. And we all have those situations, these experiences and memories that we don't ever see coming. Why don't we see them coming? Because we are too busy smothering our great "what could be" *wonder* with negative "what if the worst happens" *worry*. We lose sleep worrying, we give up minutes, hours, days, weeks of our lives to it—but for what, exactly? I couldn't have guessed in a million years what awaited me in that penthouse in New York or on that street corner in Brazil. We have the power to *wonder* excitedly about what is to come, but it's impossible to embrace that when we are caught up *worrying* over worst-case scenarios. I've heard 98% of what we worry about never ends up happening, but that might be on the low end—I'm going 99.9%.

We all worry. Even when we know it doesn't do us any good at all. We put ourselves through strife and agony, thinking about the unknowable unknown. We allow it to rob us of our daily joy. We lay awake at night worrying about the days to come—how we are going to pay our bills, keep our kids safe, make sure we get that promotion by the end of the year, etc. We even worry that we worry too much. It's a crazy mind game we play with ourselves.

So, *stop playing it.*

I know, you're thinking, "Well, we have to worry, that's just how life is."

Life . . . for who? You and everyone else you know? Small sample size. Do the birds in the sky worry about where they are going to get food tomorrow? God takes care of them daily; won't He also take care of you?

I know there is something bigger out there than me, and not having the weight of the world on my shoulders like everything depends on me (because it doesn't!) is the ultimate freedom. I love control, but, frankly, I'm not qualified to handle it and neither are you. Stop pretending you're at the wheel, and appreciate—fully appreciate and *wonder* over—the masterful control you see all around you, rather than *worrying* over things you cannot change.

No matter what you believe in, believe in something bigger than yourself. You will see the difference; you will find yourself worrying less and wondering more. You will sleep better at night, marveling over the great experience directly ahead of you.

It's really not that hard, it just takes some practice. Remind yourself daily about this mindset pivot—*wonder over worry*. You only have to choose to stop *worrying* about things outside of your control to free yourself up to experience all the *wonders* that even the most mundane aspects of daily life have to offer. Worry creates stress; wonder creates imagination and innovation. Worry is unbelief. Wonder is belief. It's all a *mindset pivot,* and it's all *your choice.*

BLUEPRINT ACTION PLAN

1. In the storm cloud on the next page, write down something you've been really worried about—something that is causing you continual stress and anguish, the thing that is keeping you up at night. In the lightning bolt, write in the absolute worst-case resolution that you can imagine—make it as dark and over-the-top as your brain will allow!

Now, in the sun, write in the absolute best-case resolution you can imagine. (Again, go as big as possible!)

Here's the fun part: When the situation does resolve, come back and write down what actually happened. I bet you anything that it is NEITHER the worst-case nor the best-case that you plotted out—I bet it's something you didn't even fully consider, something you couldn't have possibly anticipated or planned for. It could very well be even BETTER than the best-case scenario you schemed up! (And I'd be shocked if it's your worst-case nightmare.) Carry the wonder and gratitude of this resolution with you, and stop trying to yank the wheel!

2. Write down "WONDER OVER WORRY—THERE IS NO WORST-CASE SCENARIO" on a notecard and tape it next to a window or door in your home that has the least favorable view, whether that's of a busy street, your peculiar neighbors, or some never-ending construction. Take the time to come up with one thing that is truly awe-inspiring, even in this view, and appreciate it each time you pass.

DAY 9
BALANCING 52.3 POUNDS OF SUGAR

MY BUDDY TED (the reformed one-upper champ) loves golf. *Absolutely loves golf.* The guy watches reruns of PGA tour events on the Golf Network from years prior. I'm not a doctor, but I'm almost positive that's a medical treatment for insomnia.

Golf is fine, I like golf. Although, to be honest, I can't fathom finishing eighteen holes. I just don't have the three hours of patience, especially since half of my game is more of a scavenger hunt than on the green. But Ted routinely carves out big sections of each weekend for golfing with "the boys." Three hours on the course, then straight to the nineteenth hole for a couple beers, a heaping plate of nachos, and BBQ wings while watching the football game? Now, that's what Ted calls a weekend well spent.

The annual "best shot" four-man weekend tournament at Ted's local golf club has always been a big event for him. He and his "boys" finished as the runners-up one year; when the next tournament rolled around, Ted was positive this was their year. As the weekend approached, Ted and his crew put in the extra work to take them over the edge—countless extra evenings spent on the driving range hitting practice balls and repetitions on the putting green. They were ready.

They were ready . . . until the Wednesday evening before.

"You guys excited for the camping trip this weekend? Two more days! I have the marshmallows and graham crackers for s'mores already packed up!" Ted's wife chirped happily across the kitchen as she prepped dinner.

Ted's kids responded with exuberance and excitement—why wouldn't they? They LOVED the annual weekend getaway to the mountains. It was one of their favorite events of the year, and probably the most quality family time they all spent together.

Ted was frozen. He didn't know anything about a camping trip. He had his tournament to play in. His wife must have gotten the weekends mixed up. That had to be it.

Ted pulled his wife aside into the living room after dinner. "I have the golf tournament this weekend," he said softly. "I can't go camping, you know I have to be there."

His wife looked crushed, confused, and disappointed. "Ted, this is the weekend *you chose*. We booked it three months ago! You sat right there in your chair, watching golf on TV, and we had an entire conversation about it."

After much back and forth, Ted's wife decided that she and the kids would start the first day of the camping trip by themselves; Ted promised to meet them Sunday late morning, immediately after the tournament.

Ted could tell his wife was upset and hurt, and his kids were obviously devastated.

Saturday morning came, and Ted's family trekked up to the mountains alone while Ted swung for victory on the golf course with his "boys." Late Sunday morning after the golf tournament

(Ted and his crew once again fell short), Ted was stuck in bumper-to-bumper traffic due to an accident on the only road leading to the campsite. He arrived to meet his family—just in time to leave. Turn right around and drive back home, alone.

The tension at the house loomed and lingered for months after; not a word was said about the camping weekend, but the memory was as thick in the air as fog. It started to take a toll on poor old Ted.

And that's where we began our coffee conversation one weekend, scorching hot mug of Americano in my hand and a latte with extra pumps of vanilla in his.

"It's 80/20," Ted said. "I have to have my *me* time. Time on the golf course with *the boys* is good for me. I need time away from the office, time away from the family. It makes me a better husband, a better father overall. Everything in balance and moderation."

Balance, moderation, 80/20 . . . if I had a dime for every time Ted used one of those terms during that coffee meeting, I would have been able to buy half the roastery.

Finally, after hearing Ted out, I asked him what the most important things in his life were.

"My wife and kids," he responded without pause.

"Then why does the 80/20 rule apply to them?" I asked.

Ted froze as if the question was in a foreign language he had to translate and unpack in his brain.

"Sorry, man," I said, "but 'balance' is complete BS."

Did that just ruffle your feathers? Because it certainly got to Ted. He sputtered and sulked while I told him a story about my own experience with balance and moderation.

See, I used to believe in "cheat days," one day a week when I could eat "whatever I wanted," break my diet, and indulge in everything. I didn't even question it, really—that's what everything around me encouraged. That's how you keep your balance, that's how you keep your sanity. *Everything in moderation*, right?

So, I had this very thought-out, carefully researched diet to meet my goals: to be as healthy as possible, maximize daily energy, and reach specific body composition targets. Throughout the week, I'd do really well, feel great, and have all the energy in the world—until I hit that cheat meal. Then I felt gross, lethargic, and my metrics would tank. It always took me a few days to get back to where I felt like I was running at my best again. And boom, I'd hit the cheat meal again and then the cheat meal would hit me again. One of the worst parts? I didn't even really *like* the cheat meal! I only ate it because that was the 80/20 balance the world said I needed.

Call me crazy, but *I like feeling great. I like having energy. I like being healthy enough to do the things I love to do.*

The cheat meal analogy doesn't only relate to eating healthy, of course; we live in a "cheat meal" society. The mentality was derailing me. I had been letting the world dictate how I acted, letting it build in excuses for me—and I snatched them up like the Krispy Kreme donuts on Sunday that I was *allowed* to have. My actions didn't line up with my passion and goals. I wasn't being *relentlessly consistent*. That was my issue, and that was Ted's issue—and that is a lot of our issues.

The world is "80/20." It's "work-life balance." It's "just one Coke per day." It's "everything in moderation." Go ahead, pay

PASSION

attention—I bet you hear something along these lines nearly every single day. You will be faced with the choice to believe it or to realize that, in all honesty, if you are passionate about something, then *balance is BS!*

What is *moderation?* What is *balance?* The terms are so vague that anything helpful they could have led us to in the past is hopelessly twisted and misconstrued into one giant excuse. Because you know what I've noticed?

No one talks about 80/20 when they are striving to be the best version of themselves, no one says "Everything in moderation" when they are immersed in their purpose in life. No one uses the idea of balance to introduce better things into their lives—they use it to justify keeping the things in their lives that are hurting them, their goals, and their futures. "Balance" could just as easily be replaced with its evil twin synonym, "excuse." You don't have to be perfect, wake up at four each morning and grind twenty hours a day to achieve your goals. That's the complete opposite of what I am saying. And sure, you are going to fall off the horse from time to time. But there is a big difference between "slip ups" (where you get back on your horse) and "built in excuses" (where you are riding the horse backwards the wrong way).

Think about this: if I drink one Coke per night, that's 365 per year, 3,650 over the next ten years. A twenty-ounce Coke has 65g of sugar. That's 23,725 grams of sugar a year: 52.3 pounds. I guess "everything in moderation" is a better slogan than "just a little poison!" But taking a daily dose of poison isn't "balance"—it's torturing yourself.

The message that the "cheat day" is the only way to sustain eating healthy throughout the week is self-defeating. That's basically like saying "I'm on a diet that will never last. I'm not going to make it a lifestyle, that's too hard, but I'll put myself through the pain of unspiced boiled chicken breasts and microwaved broccoli throughout the week so I can indulge one day on the weekend and lose all the benefits." That just sounds miserable in every way!

YOUR GOALS ARE SUPPOSED TO BE JOYOUS! If you don't like your diet, your family, or your job enough to be ALL IN, figure out what you have to do to change the dynamic. The reason you prefer cake to microwaved broccoli is because microwaved broccoli is gross. Guess what? There are SO MANY healthy, delicious alternatives—and that holds true for every "balancing" act we do. Do we really need to go golfing with "the boys" every weekend just because we have for the past five years? Do we really have to clock in and out of our family lives like we do at the office? NO!

I want to be the best version of myself all the time because it makes me feel good and I gain the peace of living as the person I was made to be. By striving to be the best me that I can be, I get to live every day with the most joyful and passionate confidence in who I am! Sure, I slip-up and fall off the horse from time to time. But I know I can get right back on and I know the direction I'm riding.

Why would I not want to be all in spending time with the ones I love and the people who are most important to me? Why wouldn't I want to be all in attacking the mission I am on in life, my passion, my purpose? Knowing how precious time is, why would I want to spend it away from the things I want to give the most to? Just to

PASSION

meet the world's 80/20 quota? Moderation and balance, you can have 'em. I'm choosing passion and diving ALL IN!

I'll leave you with this, the same thing I texted Ted after our coffee meet-up, from my favorite person in history—Jesus:

Revelations 3:15-16: "I know your deeds; you are neither cold nor hot. How I wish you were one or the other! So because you are lukewarm—neither hot nor cold—I am about to spit you out of My mouth!"

80/20 is the definition of lukewarm.

Are you lukewarm?

BLUEPRINT ACTION PLAN

1. Fill in the first dinner plate with the unhealthy things you binge on. Whether you stuff yourself with working too many hours, stressing over the future, or piles of junk food, scribble it all in here.

   Fill the second plate with the things you have done in the name of balance and moderation. What do your "cheat days" look like? Are they full of "retail therapy" (frantically buying stuff you don't need that sets you further away from your financial goals) or golf outings or overstuffed meals?

   Take a look at your first plate and your second. This is your current diet—binging on unhealthy, un-fun stuff, and trying to reward yourself for it with unhealthy, more fun stuff occasionally. No wonder you feel gross!

   Now, fill the third plate with something in your life you want to be ALL IN on. It could be spending time with your kids, it could be helping out at your local animal shelter, it could be following your vision for a project for the benefit to others around you.

   Throw out those first two plates, and dig in to the third—that's where you're going to find the nourishment you need!

2. Write down "BALANCE IS BS" on a notecard and tape it to the cabinet where you keep your dinner plates. Reflect on what you're 100% committed to every time you open the cabinet to grab a plate.

DAY 10

THE BEST CRUISE YOU'LL NEVER REMEMBER

"DID YOU ENJOY YOUR CRUISE?"

"Yeah, Cancun was pretty good. It was fun. Wasn't as clean as I thought it would be, though."

Or, "Cozumel was enjoyable, just not as great as I had imagined it would be."

Try it out. Ask someone about a cruise they've gone on—90% of the time, the review is underwhelming. Not bad, but not great either. Not what you would expect—or that they expected.

Why is that? Isn't a cruise supposed to be one of the most enjoyable experiences, a dream vacation? Well, it's all about how you look at it—it really requires a complete mindset pivot from how we're taught to think about goals and happiness. The thing is, a cruise isn't about the destination; it's about the journey to get there. It's not about Cancun or Cozumel, it's about spending time with loved ones, relaxing and recharging, enjoying great food, maybe even seeing a comedy or magic show—not whatever ports you dock in. It's a great time if you're there for the journey itself. It's also a great metaphor for life—because when we are so caught up in the destination and where we *think* we want to be, we miss the entire purpose—the journey, the experience, the actual *where we are now*.

How often have you reached a goal you have been striving for—a promotion, a huge win, a real *life event*—and it felt kind of ho-hum? You didn't get the extravagant rush of "I've made it, now I can relax" that you thought you would. Trust me, it's not just you—it's like that for everyone. Fulfillment is reserved for our ultimate destination (which I believe is eternal life in Heaven); no earthly, fleeting riches are going to bring us that.

I religiously watched *Where in the World is Carmen San Diego?* when I was growing up. Sitting in my PJs on Saturday mornings with mouthfuls of Cinnamon Toast Crunch, I set out on the same mission as the main character—to travel all over the world.

Fast forward through my childhood, awkward adolescence, and into my twenties, and I schemed up a "fail-proof" plan to travel to thirty countries in five years. (I'm not quite sure why I chose thirty, but I knew people would be impressed.) I reached that summit sitting atop The Peak, the highest point on Hong Island. I looked over the entire country of Hong Kong, admiring the breathtaking skyscrapers aligned perfectly within the tropical forests and beautiful rolling mountains. Pure serenity.

I had made it.

So why was I feeling so underwhelmed and empty?

If you would have asked me right then and there to name all thirty countries I had been to, there was probably a 0.01% chance I would have been able. I'd been so caught up in the end result that I'd forgotten to soak in the journey. Sure, I had great adventures and amazing stories to tell from my travels, but during those five years, I could never truly rest my mind. I always had a voice

FAILURE

chirping in my ear, telling me I had to get to the next country, and then the next country, and then the next. I wouldn't be *happy* until I reached my goal.

Think about it: most people never leave the state they were born in, let alone their country. And here I was, traveling throughout the world to all of these amazing places, yet I never actually saw any of it. The Colosseum in Rome? I glanced at it passing by. The Great Wall of China? I saw it from a distance. Christ the Redeemer Statue in Rio De Janeiro? I noticed the outline from the airplane. I never took the time to explore these enchanting worlds, never took the time to fully embrace the cultures I was in. To me, life became another stamp on the passport.

My moment of clarity and understanding came on a super-hot January day in Sydney (Southern Hemisphere, so yeah, January is hot—extremely hot), as I was tackling another goal—my quest towards a million dollars. I was just finishing the second week of a tour running basketball camps in Australia; I'd been all over Melbourne the week before. I love Australia—I love the people, I love the passion for basketball, and I love the kids' excitement every time they came to camp. But these two weeks had been a grueling experience. I kept pushing through; a voice in my head reminded me, over and over, "David, you get to the end of these two weeks and you will have made $25,000! That's the largest amount of money you have ever made in two weeks—you have arrived!"

Finally, I blew the whistle for the last time. I gave my spiel to the kids about goals and never letting anyone tell them they can't achieve what they set their minds and hearts to, and then it was over.

I had reached another summit. I had made it.

So why did I feel like the life had just been deflated out of me? Wasn't I supposed to feel excited, joyful, overcome with happiness? After all, the great payday was coming my way!

I sat at my favorite coffee shop north of Sydney, in the suburb of Crow's Nest, and I let my mind wander. Without knowing it or controlling it, I thought back to one of the very first basketball camps I'd ever run, in Kirksville, Missouri, for the middle school girls' team. I ran through the entire journey, from the countless emails I had drafted, sitting outside on my parents' patio making call after call, to finally hearing "Yes, you can come do a shooting camp for our program" from the coach, to packing basketballs in my trunk and hitting the road. I stood on that court and blew the whistle for the first time, no idea what I was about to do, but standing firm and confident, acting like I had already done it a million times. And at the end of that memorable day, when the coach handed me a check for $1,000, I was beyond elated.

Sure, that check more than doubled my financial net-worth, but that joy didn't have anything at all to do with the money. It had everything to do with the joy of the journey to get to that point. Not the end result—the journey. And I enjoyed every step of it.

As I finished my long black coffee (the Aussie term for an Americano), I smiled, took a deep breath in, and just began to laugh. What I realized, at that moment, was anything but crazy. *Life isn't about what we achieve, it isn't about the end goal we are shooting for, it's about the journey and the process of getting there.* And if we don't enjoy it along the way, we've missed the entire point.

FAILURE

When we first met, James McAdoo was considered the classic example of why players *should* leave early for the NBA when they have the chance. James had been a highly regarded McDonald's All-American recruit for the North Carolina Tar Heels. After a very solid freshman season, he was projected to be a lottery pick (top thirteen) in the upcoming NBA draft. Being a lottery pick means you are a guaranteed multi-millionaire with a minimum of three years in the NBA. Seems like a no-brainer, right? Not to James—he decided to return for his sophomore season. After a similar campaign his sophomore year, James was projected to be a first-round pick in the next NBA draft; once again, he'd be guaranteed a three-year contract. He'd probably lose out on some of the millions from the year before, but he'd still be a guaranteed multi-millionaire.

Instead, James returned for his junior season.

What on earth is he thinking, you are probably wondering. Trust me, I did as well. Especially after he then underperformed against expectations. He entered the NBA draft the next summer and went *undrafted*. No money, no guaranteed contract—nothing. Just the hope that what he *missed out* on wouldn't come back to bite him in the end.

This was the point where our paths crossed for the first time, at the NBA Summer League in Las Vegas. His agent hired me to help James make the NBA and make the roster for the Golden State Warriors. I knew James's entire story inside and out before I met him at the Whole Foods on Charleston Street, north of the Vegas Strip. All of me expected James to be down-and-out, in a "woe is me" state of mind.

And all of me couldn't have been more wrong. James was extremely joyful, full of life and energy. He couldn't stop commenting on how he hadn't been to Whole Foods before and how good the strawberry banana smoothie was.

Caught off guard by James's whole persona, I went into listening-mode instead of interrogation-mode. I simply asked him his goals.

"Enjoy every day."

I figured this was the answer his agent had drilled into him, so I just kept going.

"Ok, so how are we going to make the Warriors, James?"

His response is frozen in time for me: "If it's in the Big Man upstairs' cards for me, then it will be. I'm just going to work my butt off and enjoy every minute of the journey."

Wow. To be twenty years old, having lost potential multi-millions, instant fame, and a guaranteed three-year NBA contract, yet to have that perspective, such genuine pure joy and contentment? I honestly didn't know how to respond.

James went on to make the Golden State Warriors and win two NBA Championships as a part of one of the best teams ever assembled in all of sports. Each time he won the championship, when his team was going absolutely nuts spraying champagne all over each other, James was just standing there in the background, smiling. His sense of joy and life fulfillment wasn't to be found at the pinnacle, it wasn't to be found in the way too big NBA Championship rings with way too many diamonds—it was in enjoying the journey. Fully embracing every day, every moment, and enjoying the gifts he had been given.

FAILURE

James and I still see each other whenever possible; we vacation together and talk all the time. He was a groomsman in my wedding. We often reminisce on that day at Whole Foods, and I'll tell him how crazy I thought he was. He always laughs, cracks a huge smile, and responds, "Now you get it, D. Now you understand."

And he's right. It's not about the peak of what we think will bring us joy and happiness here on this Earth; there is no "I made it moment" for fleeting, manufactured worldly goals. It's ALL about the journey, and enjoying the journey we are on.

Of course, James had the choice of returning to the Warriors after winning two championships. Everyone expected him to—who would walk away from a streak like that? Well, James, obviously. He chose to experience the journey from a different perspective. James went to Torino, Italy, and Istanbul, Turkey, where he's playing professionally overseas and raising a family while traveling through Europe, like he had always dreamed of doing. He took his own path, despite all expectations, for the same reason he didn't leave North Carolina after his freshman year—his goals aren't *summit-based*, they are *journey-based*.

Are you enjoying your daily journey or are you just trying to get to the next summit? I can tell you this much—once you reach your summit, there will always be another, even higher and harder to reach. The summit will never fill you; it will never be enough. But if you understand that the joy is in the journey, the summits will be much sweeter—sweeter than a strawberry banana smoothie from Whole Foods or a piña colada on the beaches of Cancun.

BLUEPRINT ACTION PLAN

1. On the island, write down what you've been thinking of as your ideal destination—the summit of your work and your dreams. What is your goal, what is the place you've been expecting to make you feel like you "made it"?

Now, in the open water, write down everything you can think of that makes the daily journey to this island enjoyable and fulfilling. Really take your time—fill up the whole ocean with everything you can think of. If it doesn't exist as part of your journey yet but the idea makes you smile, is there a way to incorporate it in?

If the island disappeared, if you never got to it, is this still the ocean you'd like to swim in every day?

My "made it" spot right now? I want *Pivot & Go* to sell a million copies! That's the island I want to visit!

What's between where I am and that island? Well, now I'm able to speak about the book and the impactful stories it is filled with, I am filled with a great sense of accomplishment, I've overcome the belief that I could never write a book, I get to travel to book signings and Q&As, and I gain more confidence that I can do anything I put my mind to! Heck, even if this book didn't happen to reach bestseller island, I'm loving swimming in these waters!

2. Write down "A CRUISE IS ABOUT THE CRUISE, NOT THE DES-TINATION" on a notecard and place it next to a picture of you and/or your family on your favorite vacation somewhere you will see it often. Commit to recall your best memory from that trip each time you pass it.

DAY 11
FOGGY MIRRORS

TELLING THE TOP ATHLETES IN the world what they should be doing is a little daunting at first, to say the least. I've had the opportunity to work with more than 150 NBA players, both on court (helping them develop their basketball skill sets) and off the court (helping them optimize their entire lives). Trust me, there have been many times along this journey where I had no idea what I was going to say, no idea how I was going to help. However, one thing I've learned (which I found out the hard way, multiple times) is that if I don't carry the presence and confidence that I believe in what I am saying, they see right through it. Even if I didn't know what I was doing, as long as whatever I said came across like I knew it was the exact thing they needed, then it became the exact thing they needed. People don't always buy into *what* you are saying; sometimes, they just buy into *how* you are saying it. And people never care about what you have to say until they know how much you care about them.

When I was brought on to the Brooklyn Nets to help the young players, there were still many veteran players on the team, including the exceptionally talented Joe Johnson. At that point, he was a nine-time All-Star who'd earned upwards of $200 million over the course of his NBA career. Joe had his rhythm, he had his routine—he was established. Normally when it comes to vets, you just let them do what they want and let them dictate the work they get in. If Joe wanted to do something, he definitely had the authority. I could tell Joe was feeling me out for the first few weeks. He was kind and caring, but he was also a little standoffish.

I thought I had everything figured out. I was twenty-seven, young, hungry, and confident (beyond where I probably should have been, given my experience). Yeah, I was feeling my own vibe a little too much. I thought it was confidence; in reality, it was definitely leaning much more heavily towards arrogance.

About a month into my tenure, as three-point shooting percentages started to rise, articles in the New York media began to percolate about the rejuvenation of the team. And a lot were giving me credit. That's when Joe decided it was time to test me out.

Now, Joe is very savvy. Even if you are familiar with the NBA, you probably don't realize his IQ for the game; it goes very underrated. In all honesty, Joe has one of the highest basketball IQs of any of the players I have ever been around.

He pulled me aside after practice (one of our first in the beautiful new Brooklyn facility overlooking the New York Harbor and the entire city skyline) with a basketball in each hand.

"Let's work."

Caught off guard but feeling cocky, I said, "Alright, let's go."

I asked him what he wanted and he just shrugged his shoulders: "What do you got? You're the coach."

Ok, I thought, *he wants a challenge.* So I dove in with a workout that was one of my go-to high intensity *sexy* workouts. Guys who

I worked with for the first time always walked away raving about this number.

I had Joe dribbling two balls while making passes out of one hand, followed by finishes at the rim and another shot after that. (That would never happen in a game—but it looked really, really cool.)

Joe went through the workout. Never asked one question. As soon as one drill was completed, he simply asked, "What you got next?"

He kept asking, so I kept bringing it. Drill after drill, until Joe was drenched with sweat and had his hands on his knees.

"That's good, that's enough for today," he commanded. He went to the free throw line, made a few to finish, and nodded to me to come meet him there.

Great! I thought, *I just gave one of the best players in the NBA my best workout, and I dominated him throughout it. He loved it! Not only can I help young players develop, but I can help nine-time All-Stars without even having to study their game.* I prepped for a big embrace and thanks.

Instead, I got an anvil to the top of the head, dropped out of the clear blue sky: "You don't know what you're doing, do you, kid?" Joe asked.

The word *kid* alone froze me in my tracks. Why was he calling me *kid?* Didn't he know I was the reason the Nets were turning around their entire franchise, the entire perception of the organization?

"I love your energy and I love your passion, but what we just did had no relevance to what I need to improve on. I would never use any of those shots in a game."

Ouch. That stung. It more than stung. Time had stopped around me.

"I like you, kid, but if you want to have a career in this league, you have to know your role. I know you want to come in here and make a difference. That's cool. We want that. I want that. But you're going about it the wrong way. Credit isn't yours for the taking. Don't be arrogant, that fire will burn out quickly and no one will want to be around you. Be confident, but not arrogant. Got it, kid?"

I just nodded. I tried to think of something to say, but I had a lump in my throat the size of the Rock of Gibraltar. He gave me a pat on the back and walked off to hit the showers. I stood in the same exact spot, legs frozen. In only an hour, I'd gone from thinking that I was *the man* to feeling as small as a mouse.

But I needed that, bad. I'd been on a collision course that would have ultimately been my downfall. Joe Johnson's hard dose of reality was a huge favor, but of course, I didn't realize it right away. I was upset with him and resented him. I tried to avoid him at all costs for the next week. But then it sunk in—Joe actually cared about me enough to give me his time and his energy, even though he knew exactly what was going to happen during that workout. He cared enough about my future to teach me the difference between confidence and arrogance and how to play my role as a servant. Joe had been watching me the entire month, and he chose the moment I needed it the most: when he knew my head was getting too big to keep on my shoulders.

That hour with Joe changed my entire perception of the work that I do. I've never again stepped onto the court thinking I was better than the person I was about to work with. I didn't lose my confidence, but I completely got rid of arrogance. I shed myself of thoughts like "How can I get players to work to my benefit?" or "How can I rack up more accolades and newspaper articles that point to me?" and replaced them with "How can I serve each player as a person and as an athlete every time I step on the floor with them?"

The *mindset pivot* NBA superstar Joe Johnson helped me make that day has not only shaped my career—it's also shaped my interactions in every realm of life. I am confident in my God-given abilities, and I am confident that I am using them for the benefit of others. I pour into others and ultimately find myself—the servant attitude. And I have Joe to thank for that.

Joe and I would talk after games for hours over catered locker room food from the Barclays Center in Brooklyn. We typically reflected on the events that occurred in the game, but every so often, we would end up reminiscing about *the* workout. Joe would crack up while jabbing me about how afraid I'd looked. I laughed along with him, much more at ease and comfortable with myself, able to enjoy a laugh at my own expense—something I never could have done before. That's right—I was able to laugh at myself. I know that seems trivial, but it felt so freeing. I was free of what I thought I had to be, and free of the arrogance I had built up on the inside with my "untouchable" approach. I had become vulnerable, in a great way. From *untouchable* to *vulnerable*. Remaining *confident* but not *arrogant*. And it was all a *mindset pivot*.

Arrogance is thinking you are better than others; confidence is believing in yourself to empower others.

In no way, shape, or form am I ever the smartest or most talented person in the room. I'm not even going to say I will outwork everyone in the room—it's not about being the last man standing. What I do know is that I am going to attack every day with *relentless consistency*—in my passion, in the belief I have in myself, and in not caring what anyone else thinks of me. Confidence is all about the perception you have of yourself. You have a clear mirror and a foggy mirror in your life. In the clear mirror, you can see yourself with confidence; the foggy mirror shows you the view distorted, riddled with self-doubt or arrogance. If you leave a mirror foggy, there is no way you can ever see your true self. It will mildew and mold, just as your attitude will if you go through life unconfidently. You have the ability to defog your mirror in every situation.

Confidence is allowing yourself to be vulnerable and *laughing at your own mistakes*. Learn from them and grow from them, but also be able to laugh at them—trust me, it will free you. Be confident in who you are, but as a servant to others. Pour into others and their needs, and in doing so, you will be filled. From that day on court with Joe Johnson, I learned that *dying* to myself and my perceived wants and desires allows me to actually, truly, fully *live*.

BLUEPRINT ACTION PLAN

1. Inside the foggy mirror, write down the things you are not fully confident in about yourself. It could be anything; for example, it could be "I am not confident because I am shy."

   Now, in the clear mirror, write down the opposite. For example, "I am confident because I am bold."

   I could easily scrawl, "I AM IMPATIENT!" all across my foggy mirror. Nothing seems to ever happen fast enough for me. I am not confident because I can't seem to get things accomplished right away. Do you even know how long it takes to write a book?!? (Turns out it's more than the three months I had slated.)

   Now, in the clear mirror, I'll write, "I am patient because I want the best result." Do you know what a wreck this book would have been written, published, and on the shelves in only three months? Luckily, I wouldn't put you through that. If I had, it would have lacked the impact I wanted it to have. I learned to be patient through the process of reading every chapter time after time after time. Through this patience, I've gained the even greater sense of accomplishment that I have put the best book out into the world that I could produce.

2. Write down "I BELIEVE IN THE POWER OF ME" on a notecard and pencil in your mirror-confident statements. Tape it to the mirror you look at first in the morning, and commit to reading the whole thing aloud to your reflection as you start your day.

DAY 12

SHOOTING LESSONS WITH MARK CUBAN

I USED TO BE A TV junkie. Not like a Netflix binge watcher; my type A personality won't allow me to sit still long enough for all that. But NBA games? LOVE 'EM. And I could justify watching every game possible, because it was part of my job . . . well, sort of. I needed to watch the players I was personally coaching, sure, but watching every game for every team was *probably* not the most efficient use of my time.

It all piled up on me at once. I was working with five high-level NBA players as their personal/life coach. I watched all their games, sent them over their personal film clips with review and analysis, helped them get mentally prepared for the next game, tracked their sleep/nutrition/recovery—basically, I made sure they were going into every game at their optimal level and that they were learning and growing on court and afterwards as well. I was hardly sleeping at night, getting up at four in the morning to do reviews for my East Coast players so they could have the feedback first thing in the morning to prepare for their next game. (God-forbid it was back-to-back games two nights in a row.)

I hadn't hung out with friends or seen family for over three months . . . I was too busy. But I wasn't too busy to watch nearly every game, sitting in front of my TV from four to ten basically every single evening. I was addicted to TV; it owned me, and the worst part was, I didn't realize it. It wasn't even helping me with my job anymore. My reviews got shorter and less in depth and my motivation and mindset coaching became relatively redundant, but I didn't notice because I was too "busy." There wasn't even close to enough time to give five players my best AND watch six hours of TV a night.

Then one day, I woke up at 4:05 AM and was greeted with a text: "Hey man, I think I'm going to focus on the games and everything else myself for a while. I just feel like I can be more prepared this way."

That felt like a dagger to the heart, if I'm being honest. I'd just lost one of my clients, but more importantly, let down a good friend I really cared deeply for. I knew he would forgive me, but I had no idea whether we'd ever truly get past this moment in our relationship. (To this day, we are friends, but not really *friends*. Everything is very cordial and surface level. And I HATE surface level!)

I decided the TV had to go. And it did. That day, I called up one of those close friends of mine that I hadn't seen for over three months and asked him if he wanted to grab dinner—dinner on me and a free TV. Not only did he accept the offer, he jumped at it.

I made a choice to take back control of my life. I decided *I* would *much rather be great than watch others be great.*

You are the sum of your relationships. It's not about what you got on your SAT, what prestigious college you went to, what you do for a job, or what type of house you live in—it's about your relationships. I make a point to stay in touch once a month with fifteen friends in my field, fifteen people who I know can help me in my personal growth, on my journey, with mentorship advice, and with overall big asks (if I ever need those). I know it might sound like I am using these fifteen people, but it's far from that. I build up the equity and friendship with these people through giving, giving, and giving some more to them without ever expecting anything in return. I care for these friends deeply, so even if I never get anything back from them, it's not a loss because *they* are gaining. It's true, genuine friendship building. As I've said, I absolutely hate the term "networking." It's way too surface level for me. It feels slimy, like one person is using the other person.

When I reach out, it's more than just a "Hey, how have you been, thinking of you," or "How are the kids doing?" I am authentically engaging with each of them in a personal, encouraging way—a way that I hope helps guide them, enriches their lives, and promotes their own passions. If I'm in Japan, for example, I will hunt down the most esoteric and out-of-the-way restaurant for my sushi foodie friend back home, a place that even if they were to visit Japan, they would probably never stumble across by themselves; I will smash sushi until I am near comatose, taking pictures of the entire experience and issuing a full review. I know very well their favorite food is authentic Japanese sushi, and if they can't be there personally, I'll give them the best experience outside of actually tasting it. It's about going the extra mile to show how much I care and value the relationship. I'll take it for the team. That's friendship. (See, you didn't know friendship could be so tasty, did you?)

I always ask if I can help them in any way. I give, give, and give some more, without ever expecting anything in return. But it's not a chore—it's a privilege! I feel most alive when I pour myself into others and know they are benefiting from what I can provide to them.

One member of my golden fifteen is a guy you've probably heard of—Mark Cuban. Mark is an absolute business tycoon, for those of you who have been living under a rock for the better part of the last decade. (Although, by the time this book hits its one millionth sale, he'll probably be the president of the United States. See how I just spoke the one millionth sale into existence?)

Anything Mark touches turns to gold. The entire world is clamoring for his attention. So, how do you get a person like Mark in your network? How do you get him to return your emails and calls? How do you even get a person like him to know you exist?

Simple; you give. You give, and give, and give some more, without ever expecting anything in return.

I'm nowhere near Mark's level, but I have dealt with a lot of people who reach out, asking to work for me; within the first twenty minutes of the conversation, the majority of these people ask how much they are going to make and what their job title is going to be. Nope, done, checked off the list. No chance they are working for me. If it's solely about the money for them, I know right off the bat they are in it for the wrong reasons. Money is great, but not when it's your driving force. When I meet people whose driving force is genuinely giving for the betterment of others, pouring into others because they care deeply, then I know I'm dealing with people who have found the magic formula—not just for business success, but for life in general. Those are the type of people I want to work with and for.

I was with the Brooklyn Nets in Dallas for a mid-season game. Both teams had less-than-great records, though Dallas's was better than ours. (To be fair, not a lot of teams had a worse record than us at that juncture!)

I always enjoyed getting out on the court extra early before the game, just as a way to soak in the atmosphere and breathe in with gratitude that I was in the NBA. But for once, I wasn't the first one on the floor.

Turns out Mark Cuban likes to get out on the court early as well. He's a basketball junkie, as clearly evidenced by his ownership of the Mavericks. And turns out he is a big fan of figuring out how he can become a better shooter.

I saw that he needed some help on his jumper, so I walked onto the court and began to make small talk while rebounding for him, watching him shoot. (And analyzing the less-than-perfect mechanics on his jumper for myself. To be completely honest, it was much better than I had expected.)

Then, the opportunity presented itself; after another missed shot, he blurted out in frustration, "I'm getting too old, the legs just aren't like they used to be."

I countered with, "You know, it's not as much about the legs as you might think."

He was visibly intrigued. "Yeah, how so?"

"It's not how much force you generate with your legs; it's

the balance and how you distribute the force that makes all the difference."

Now, I had his ear; he knew I was an expert in something that he wanted to improve upon. I knew I had him hooked, so I continued to give: "Mind if I show you a couple pointers that I think could help you out?"

"I'm all ears," he replied, palms in the air in surrender.

I went on to give him a quick fifteen-minute tutorial with a couple of my go-to points that would help him immediately better his shot and generate power in his legs through triple extension of his ankles, knees, and hips (so he wouldn't actually have to jump high). I knew it would make a notable difference in the distance the ball traveled and the actual effort he had to put into getting the ball to the rim.

He ate it up. As players started to come on the court for their pre-game workouts, I told him I had much more info I could send him, and I asked for his email. He was interested in what I had and what it could do for him, so he gave me his email and told me to follow up.

To this day, I have no idea who even won that game (I'm pretty sure the Mavericks did); I was too enamored with what had just happened to actually pay much attention. I followed up with Mark the next day, showing that I was very interested in helping him, and within five minutes of sending him the first email, he responded. Mission accomplished.

I gave and gave shooting tips to him without asking for anything in return; what it led to was far more fruitful than anything

I could have thought to ask for. I built a relationship with one of the most powerful businesspeople on the entire planet, a genuine relationship that turned into a friendship. Now, I reach out to him and he reaches out to me, and it all started because I gave without expecting anything in return.

That's the *mindset pivot*—when you are able to fully pour into and lose yourself in the genuine care of others, that is when you find out who you truly are. Lose yourself to find yourself.

I challenge you to make a list of your Golden 15; fifteen people you should stay in touch with regularly, who can help you grow in your journey and as an overall better person. Give, give, and give some more. Without expecting anything in return. And be creative with your gifts. Don't just do what everyone else might do. Put time and effort into those gifts; give the best parts of yourself. Make these gifts original, make them yours. Don't just give a gift card. Show the time, effort, and value you put into these relationships—trust me, you will reap the benefits.

BLUEPRINT ACTION PLAN

1. On the next page, list your Golden 15—both their names and one thing that you know is personally significant to them. Make a habit of reaching out to them in some way on a regular basis with a text or a call (something that is definitely not overbearing, but genuinely shows them that you care and you are there to serve them). Start brainstorming creative tokens of your admiration and appreciation that you know they'll love!

2. Write down "LOSE YOURSELF TO FIND YOURSELF" on a notecard and place it in a highly visible spot where you do the majority of your work during the day. Each time you see it, take a few moments to think of something meaningful you can do for one of your Golden 15.

1

2

3

4

5

6

7

8

YOU

9

10

11

12

13

14

15

DAY 13
PUZZLE PIECE PROBLEMS

DOMAS SABONIS. YOU MIGHT KNOW the NBA star for his performance on the court; if you're a real basketball nut, you might know him as the son of the NBA all-time great Ardvyonous Sabonis. Domas was gifted with natural athletic ability and height, but when you come from a name like Sabonis, you need to be good—no, you need to be GREAT. And Domas . . . well, he wasn't.

For the average Lithuanian, basketball is life—the way NFL football is to the most die-hard Sunday American football-nut you've ever met. From a young age, Domas was held up as the golden child of Lithuania, the one who would bring the country back to basketball prominence. But Domas struggled, to the point that everyone began to wonder if he would ever live up to his father's legacy.

That burden wore on Domas; he wanted to be great so badly. By the time he arrived at Gonzaga University, the game he loved had become more of a burden than a passion. He was no longer as excited as he'd once been to play, and he was driving himself crazy— throwing up from anxiety and fighting teammates to let out anger. He was so worked up, he struggled making a shot a foot away from the hoop. Domas was at a breaking point. There was no enjoyment or pleasure in his daily life anymore, just the overwhelming grind.

Then, Domas was given a gift that changed absolutely everything for him. The Gonzaga assistant coach (who had been by Domas' side since he'd started recruiting him at sixteen) allowed Domas to embrace being bad at something. He taught Domas how to laugh at himself for failing. Domas was no longer yelled at for missing free throws, and he learned to stop yelling at himself. It was a complete 180 degree pivot from what coaches typically preach to players—PERFECTION, PERFECTION, PERFECTION! Domas had the permission to fail and have fun doing so.

I spent a lot of time with Domas over the summer of 2018. I watched him walk on to the court every morning at ten, having already worked on his conditioning, stretching and flexibility, and weights. By this time, Domas had a potential enormous NBA contract extension looming, the Olympic qualifying hopes of his country resting on his broad shoulders, and the up-and-coming franchise of the Indiana Pacers counting on him—all the reasons in the world to feel burdened by expectations. But he would always come into the gym as if he didn't have a worry in the world. Sun-drenched blonde hair and huge smile illuminating the entire gym of Santa Monica, like David Hasselhoff stepping directly out of a *Baywatch* scene, Domas would say hello to everyone; his calmness and peace made it seem like he had spent the entire last week on the beaches in the Maldives.

I'd ask him what he was going to work on for the day, and the response was the same each time: "Just going to try to get a little better today, and going to have a lot of fun trying."

At the end of many of our workouts, Domas would say, "Man,

I was bad today"—followed by a laugh and a huge smile. Then, he would quickly move on with his day.

In the past, the frustration of bad workouts, missing shots, or not meeting the expectations of others ate him up. But Domas let himself be bad, even at something he knew he was great at. And in the process, he became better than maybe he could have ever imagined. Not only was he one of the most improved players in the NBA that season, he was one of the most enjoyable people on the face of the planet to be around. The peace he had was contagious to everyone around him.

Domas understood the answer to one of life's hardest riddles, something that causes enormous stress in most lives—how to enjoy the daily grind. He'd figured out the formula: allow yourself to be bad at what you do great and be comfortable laughing at yourself.

We put so much into what we do that it defines us—but there is always that person in our lives who could care less and is still better than us at it. How does that happen? Because they don't attach their identity to the results, that's how. The thing that we think defines us doesn't define them. They have perspective on the issues that arise, which allows them to work towards solving problems without questioning the core of who they are. Basketball greatness defined Domas Sabonis. But he didn't find true greatness until he detached himself from that identity.

I could tell you that you are going to live your best day and be the best version of yourself every day, that you will wake up every morning with ultimate joy, passion for what you do, and overall confidence in who you are. I could pump motivation straight into your veins. With some luck, it might stick—for a week, a month, maybe even a year. But when the shiny luster wears off, when you hit a particularly grueling time, one morning, you would once again open your eyes and think, "Do I really have to go through this day again?" There are always going to be moments where you feel the grind of life pulling you down, pulling you back into that bed. No matter what I say or what you believe, one day, you will want to pull those covers back over your head and hide from the world. No matter how many sunny days we can string together in a row, there will always come a point where we face another thunderstorm inside ourselves.

As much as I LOVE waking up every morning excited to take on the day, I'd be lying through my teeth if I told you I didn't have times where I thought, "Yep, today's going to be like getting a root canal." And I'll try to placate myself with all kinds of motivational words and sayings, all sorts of deep breathing and gratitude practices, multiple cups of my favorite coffee in my favorite mug, and reinvigorating workouts—but still, the reality of the daily grind of life will weigh down on me like an unmovable mountain. Even though I love my life and my mission, every moment of every day isn't the most fun I've ever had.

We spend a lot of time looking for the WHY (why are we here?) and the WHAT (what is our purpose?), assuming that when we find answers for those, the whole HOW (how do we enjoy the everyday grind of life?) will just kind of clear itself up. It won't, but by pivoting our mindsets, we can come to a better understanding and appreciation of that HOW.

Do you remember how riveting puzzles were when you were

younger? No matter how big it was, even if the picture on the box wasn't anything to get excited about, it was still thrilling, making those pieces fit in the exact right spots. You were creating something beautiful and complete out of something broken. When you were convinced the piece you needed just hadn't been included in the box, you would sometimes keep hunting for it, laughing as you went through the stacks. Most times, though, you moved on to another piece, knowing that the "missing" one would turn up eventually. That puzzle was an exciting challenge, not a problem you couldn't overcome. You enjoyed the journey and the process, and you knew there was a beautiful picturesque end in sight.

I was almost thirty years old on the day my younger brother got engaged in 2016. My older sister was already married, with one kid and another on the way. And then there was me, the middle child, about the furthest from married as could be. Not because I didn't want to be. Sure, I always envisioned myself being married, but nothing happens from just imagining something—you must actively pursue and desire it.

That day, I decided it was time—time I stopped being so caught up in my career pursuits, so that I could take the steps to getting married.

It's an interesting thing about life: when you force something and try to manipulate all the variables because you want it so bad, it never ends up actually happening. But when you put yourself in the right situation, the right frame of mind, and let God's timing do the work, that's when everything falls into place, exactly like puzzle pieces.

So there I was, dating any prospect I met. If I met a girl at church or at the gym, I'd be on a date with her within the week. I figured if I met someone in a place that I enjoyed, then there would have to be similarities and sparks between us, right?

Wrong!

But did that stop me from trying to force an authentic connection?

Nope!

In fact, I forced it so much that I landed on an ABC reality dating show called *The Love Connection*. Yeah, it got that bad. And it didn't stop there. I'm not proud to admit it, but I was even a finalist to be on *The Bachelor*. My pursuit of a soulmate had consumed me to the point that I was trying anything and everything to make the corner-shaped puzzle pieces fit into the middle.

Then, I got to the point in a longer relationship where I almost settled. I would constantly look past the obvious red flags because I had put on the society blinders: I *needed* to get married. I tried to find compatibility where there was none. All of my gut intuition told me it was wrong, but the voice constantly echoing in my head said, "This is what life is about: making sacrifices. You can't have everything you want in a life partner; you have to concede in some areas." That was the lie I was telling myself. And I almost bought it.

If we are being completely honest with ourselves, a lot of us do this. Start from square one again in my thirties? No way, that's too daunting. I'll just get married to someone I'm not crazy about because everyone says the honeymoon stage never actually lasts anyways. Great relationships come from the difficult times, right?

SUCCESS

Wrong. Absolutely wrong. But I almost fell for these lies.

One summer evening, I came back to my apartment after another long and draining argument with the girl I was trying to force myself to be compatible with. I dropped my hopeless body on the couch, sprawled out, and yelled out at the top of my lungs, "I QUIT."

I probably scared the life out of my roommate, Rich, but less than ten seconds later, he was hovering over me and laughing. (Trust me, I didn't think it was funny.)

"Why don't you quit trying so hard?" Rich asked. "Let go and let God."

Now I believe in God and I believe He can make anything happen. But I didn't believe He was ever going to just give me my soulmate. I thought it all depend on me. I thought that, just like everything else in my life, I had to make it happen.

But therein lies the problem: I was depending all on myself to make this wife thing happen like it was a deadline I had to rush to hit.

"Breathe," Rich said with a smirk on his face as I laid in a heap of frustration. "The right one is out there; it's just a matter of time before you find her. But it will never happen if you force it. You're stressing me out just looking at you!"

He was right. More than right.

I looked at my situation as a problem—my little brother (six years younger than me!) was getting married, most of my friends were married, so why couldn't I find the one for me?

But the words "Let go and let God" sunk in. Nothing I had ever wanted in my career had happened overnight; nothing had happened by trying to force it. It had all happened because I'd prepared for the opportunity with persistence and patience, with the knowledge that it would all work out at the exact right time it was supposed to work out. Not on my timing, but God's timing—a much better time than I could even imagine.

At that moment, a weight was lifted off my shoulders. No longer did I feel pressured to meet the nonexistent marriage deadline I had created, or to stay in a mediocre relationship, or to go on reality TV dating shows. (Which I won, by the way. If you want a really good laugh, search my name and *Love Connection* online and get the tissues ready . . . for laughing tears, not crying!)

Not even three months after the night that I decided to give up any sort of manipulation to find "the one," I found her. And the first moment she walked across the street to me at The Coffee Bean & Tea Leaf, I knew I would spend the rest of my life with her. I'd never believed people who said, "When you know, you know." But trust me, I knew.

And the rest is history. Now I'm married to that amazing girl with the smile that stopped my heart. And without her, I wouldn't be close to the person I am today. Shoot, you wouldn't be reading this book right now! She supports me in everything I do, she loves me unconditionally, she cares for me, she is my best friend, she is my everything. Literally my everything.

And it would have never happened unless I "let go and let God."

The ironic thing about this whole story? My roommate Rich was the one who set me up with her. It's almost like he knew I had to go through my personal struggle to pivot from problems to puzzles before I could fully appreciate everything.

In adult life, we create our own daily grind by holding onto the expectations we have for ourselves so tightly that we're always on the verge of breaking. We must succeed, we must get the promotion, we must drive the nice car, we must be considered the best at what we do. Those burdens build up, though maybe not on the outside (we are ALL great at putting on our masks and covering up the real us). But the deeper we push those expectations inside of us, the more we numb ourselves to the joy of the daily find. Instead of looking at each day as the daily grind, we can pivot to seeing it as the daily find. The find is the missing piece that makes the puzzle beautiful and whole. But if we fail to appreciate the puzzles in our lives, which are full of possibilities and solutions, then we turn them into problems that we just have to grind through.

And that's the one-word mindset pivot you have to make: *grind* into *find*. Such a minor adjustment that has such major consequences! You make puzzles out of your problems, and you learn to laugh at yourself, and you pick up the pieces as you can. No one piece is your entire identity; they are all parts of building your completed, beautiful picture. And when you can't find one piece, you hunt for the others, trusting that everything will come together when the time is right.

BLUEPRINT ACTION PLAN

1. In the puzzle piece on the next page, write down one part of the daily grind that you've been dreading—the worst, the part of life you feel you've really been failing at. That's your puzzle piece of the day—you're really going to hunt for that one! And you're going to be bad at it! You're going to allow yourself to be bad at it, to try it and put your effort in, and stink up the court. Put your all into it today, and if it doesn't happen, that's okay too—keep preparing yourself for the day that piece turns up, and start working on the other pieces in your life!

    Something that I need to allow myself to be bad at? I actually had trouble coming with this one, so I asked my wife . . . that was a mistake. She was able to come up with a top five! If you're having problems, ask someone close to you. Trust me, they'll think of something!

    My biggest struggle is feeling like I haven't accomplished enough, hence why I "overwork." Trust me, that's not a good thing. Following your passion and being on a mission is GREAT, but when it comes at the expense of the most important things in your life, then it's an issue. I need to be able to just take a deep breath and laugh at myself when I don't get as much done in a day as I would have liked. And that's just one of many on my wife's list for me!

2. Write down "LIFE IS A DAILYFIND, NOT A GRIND" on a notecard and tape it above the spot where you prepare your morning coffee (or whatever your favorite morning drink is). Commit to reflecting on how well your day is starting off as you take your first sip each morning and capture a good laugh to bring out when you run into something that frustrates you.

DAY 14
THE BEACH FRONT PATIO

IN 2014, THE BROOKLYN NETS made a devastating trade—maybe the worst one in NBA history. Ransacked of talent, they needed to build the culture of their new franchise. They were depending on some of their young players to perform at a level that most aren't remotely expected to perform at in the early stages of their careers. On top of that, the Nets were next to dead last in three-point shooting percentage—twenty-eighth in the NBA, to be exact.

They decided there was only one guy who could help them turn it all around—me! (Ok, that's me being maybe a little over-confident, but hey, they asked me for a reason, right?) Here I was at twenty-seven, the young hot up-and-comer, one of the top-regarded shooting coaches in the world. All my NBA dreams and daily preparation on the court led me here. Now, I had the opportunity to revive an entire NBA franchise—we're literally talking about a dream job BETTER than my original dream! Not only had I made it, but if I did well, I could write my own ticket in the NBA—any role I wanted, for life.

So, you're probably wondering, *how did it go?*

AMAZING!

Right from the jump, we were rocking. In the first three games of my tenure, the Nets set the record for most threes made in a game. The media latched on to the story, releasing article after article about the new shooting coach "changing the landscape in Brooklyn."

That twenty-eighth place in three-point shooting? I guess you could say we improved a little by the end of the season —to second in the league!

Brooklyn was buzzing with expectation and excitement for the future, and I was set. I was expecting a great contract extension; I was even promised a three-year deal that would basically set me up for life. Three years? In three years, we would undoubtedly be one of the best teams in the NBA! Could life get any better?!? Seriously, this was everything I had ever wanted, and now I had it locked down for good. The NBA life was mine. Forever.

At the end of the season, new management came in. That always makes people a little nervous, especially because there were going to be some changes to the coaching staff. Big ones—like a new head coach. But I was golden, the Nets's "saving grace," and management told me how much they respected the work I did with the players.

The season ended, and I had just enough time to run back to my home state of Iowa and run my basketball camps before I needed to report back to Brooklyn to start the off-season development and NBA pre-draft training. Like I said, I had it made—not only was I developing the current players, but I was helping to make decisions on who we would be drafting.

A month went by, and we were deep into off-season development when Kenny Atkinson was officially hired as the head coach. I knew Kenny from past NBA Summer Leagues—not well, but well enough to know he was a development coach at heart, like me. He'd also worked very closely with one of my best friends—

Jeremy Lin. I knew Jeremy was putting in the call to hype me up to Kenny before we even stood on the same court. You know, in case he'd somehow missed all the amazing press coverage . . . the massive improvements to our shooting averages . . . and the contract extension the new GM had already promised me.

Okay, I'll admit it—I was a little worried. I knew absolutely everything was on my side, but what if the unthinkable happened? I was living the dream, and there was really only one guy who could take it away with a snap of his fingers. I'd had doors slam in my face before—what if it happened again?

Kenny arrived, and . . . everything was fine. I was still leading the development workouts, and we were looking good. I know, it was silly to even worry, right? You've seen a horror movie or two—you know when you're sure something bad is lurking around the corner . . . and the hero walks towards it . . . and there's nothing there? Such relief!

But then, without warning, the evil pops around the other corner and chaos ensues . . .

The morning that the GM brought in his best friend to run the development workouts was the jumpscare in my horror flick. What? Where did this come from? Who was this guy?!? In a daze, I jogged up and down the court in my new role as the glorified rebounder and water boy.

I recovered quickly. I knew what I needed to do: I had to keep being myself. I had to put in 110% on the court, the way I always had, without worrying about the results. I had to give the new coaching staff time to see what I could do.

I was still on the court with one of the future star players for the

Nets, working hard and working late, when my phone started ringing. I finally ran over, mid-workout, to see who was calling. It was the GM.

"Nurse," he said. He paused and swallowed hard. It was already about as uncomfortable as a phone call can be. "We're going to have to let you go."

Those words.

Crushed.

You've heard them before, or some variation: *we need to break up*, or *this isn't working out*, or *you have to leave*. Rejection usually stings, but when it's something you wanted so bad, it's the worst feeling. You just stand there with the knife firmly planted in your ribs, knowing someone doesn't think you are good at what you do, someone doesn't want you, you're not appreciated, as you watch all of your goals and dreams vanish into thin air.

"Kenny wants to move in a different direction and clear house of anyone who was here on staff before him."

I was shocked; my thoughts were spinning out of control. Wasn't I David Nurse, one of the top shooting coaches in the world, the one who was playing an enormous role in reviving the Nets, taking them from one of the worst shooting teams in the NBA to one of the best? What about my three-year contract? Was this really happening? It didn't make sense.

So, I mustered up everything that I had and I laid out the facts. I called the head coach and laid into him for not having the nerve to talk to me himself. Then I charmed him into not only keeping me, but promoting me.

I'm kidding. I squeaked out a "Really?" And that was it. End of conversation.

I was shaken to my core. The door had slammed so hard in my face that I couldn't do anything except slowly fall backwards until my head hit the pavement. I was broken. My dream job, gone in an instant, and nowhere to turn. It was already the middle of the off-season; every other NBA team had their coaches in place. There was no future for me in Brooklyn—no future I could reasonably foresee in the NBA at all. At twenty-eight, as quickly as it had started for me, it was over. Gone.

At times like this, people try to comfort us with thoughts like, "When one door closes, another opens." Whatever. It sounds like a bunch of BS—because it is!

The phrase should actually be: "When one door closes, four other doors open and so does a beach front patio overlooking the ocean."

When we get rejected and slammed to the ground, when that knife feels hopelessly buried between our ribs—when all we can hear is "you're not good enough"—that's when we find out we're even better than we imagined.

You never lose your dream job—you lose the jobs you *thought* were your dream. You don't get dumped by your soulmate—you get dumped by the people you *thought* were your soulmates. That rejection is a helping hand guiding you to your actual destiny. That rejection is the best way of finding out what you really want and what you have really been put on this earth for.

I swear by it, because I live it. Fast forward from that awful call to the present day, nearly five years removed. I'm thirty-two, and I wake up every morning with extreme joy to attack the day ahead, inspired by the mission I am on and confident in who I am. I have found and built a new career that stems from my true passions—speaking, motivating, helping people learn who they are at the core and how to be completely confident in their own skin. Making that happen has been so much more fulfilling for me and so much more beneficial for others than watching three-point shooting percentages rise a couple of points. I've developed closer, more genuine relationships with NBA players, who seek me out as a basketball development expert *and* as a mentor and life coach. I have traveled to over fifty countries, and I come home to the beach in Los Angeles—literally, I walk out my front door every morning onto a patio overlooking the ocean. I'm married to the most amazing woman I could ever imagine, I create my own schedule, and everything is better than I ever dreamed.

But none of this would have happened if that door in Brooklyn hadn't been slammed in my face. I'm so grateful now for that day, for that call. I'm grateful because it *did* end that part of my life. If that hadn't happened, I would have never figured out what I truly wanted and what I was truly destined for. The life I have now blows anything I could have done on my old path way out of the water.

Some of us will only have one door close on us and some of us will have many, but each one is a gift. Once you embrace that, you don't have to spend any time staring at slammed doors, no time wallowing on the concrete. Pivot your mindset and slide that beachfront patio door open—because once you do, the view is beyond anything you could ever imagine!

BLUEPRINT ACTION PLAN

1. Inside door #1, write down the last time you felt really shut down. The fresher, the better—what's still got you reeling, at least a little?

Now, pivot to door #2. Write down another situation, further in the past, when it seemed like a door to your dreams slammed.

Take the time to really think about door #2; after it closed, what opportunities did you discover? I know you're going to come up with a bunch—just write down your strongest three in the right-hand column.

Okay, shift back to door #1, and give it just as much thought. If you're struggling to come up with a list of benefits, that's fine—in fact, that's great! That means you haven't found your patio door yet. Get pumped (I know I'm excited for you!) and write down the three most incredible things you can possibly imagine coming from this redirection.

Take a close look at this list—this is a great gift from the not-so-gentle guiding hand of rejection, the start of a real roadmap to where you actually need and want to go.

2. Write down "WHEN ONE DOOR CLOSES, FOUR OPEN ALONG-SIDE A BEACHFRONT PATIO OVERLOOKING THE OCEAN" on a notecard and tape it next to the window or door in your home that reflects the best view. Commit to appreciating that view each time you pass it.

DAY 15
PIZZA TIME

IT HAD BEEN A LITTLE while since my buddy Ted and I had been able to get together for coffee, but the moment we sat down, I could tell something heavy was weighing on him.

"How do you have time to do everything you do?" Ted asked.

I paused, caught off guard by the abrupt question. Not even a "Hey man, how you doing?" I also didn't really know how to respond. There didn't seem to be a good answer—I'd always just figured I did so much because I was wired like the Energizer Bunny with that "do, do, do, do" gene (a blessing and a curse).

Ted went on to tell me that he felt stuck. He said he'd woken up one morning and realized ten years had passed him by, just vanished. He wasn't anywhere close to living out his dream. And the thing he'd once been so positive he'd do after college wasn't happening. He didn't know how he had gotten to this point. Sure, he loved his wife and his kids, but he was stuck in a rut and didn't know how to get out.

Well, I knew I'd need more clues than the Grand Canyon-sized term 'rut'!

I asked him what a normal day looked like. He told me he would wake up, make coffee, read the *Kansas City Star*, check golf highlights on his phone, see the kids at breakfast, drive to work, sit at his desk until six, drive home, eat dinner with the family, watch golf highlights, go to bed, rinse, and repeat it all over again the next day.

I literally cringed. There was nothing wrong with any of the individual elements of his day, but when you added them all up, there wasn't any excitement or adventure either. I'm not talking bare-knuckle boxing or top-secret-007 assassin excitement—where was the "camping out with the kids in the front lawn" or "waking up early to go for a sunrise hike with the family" adventure? Or the "take the wife out to an intimate dinner in the city" surprise? Ted was surviving the day-to-day, keeping his head above water, instead of looking at each and every day as one to embrace and enjoy.

Ted, in short, had a major problem with his pizza.

Now, you might be thinking, "Woah, what the heck is David Nurse, the absolute health and wellness nut, doing talking about pizza? And pizza problems, at that?"

Well, pizza technology has come a long way in my lifetime. We no longer live in a world of pepperoni, sausage, or vegetables. From cauliflower crusts to basil pesto sauces to eggs and truffle pecorino, the 800 Degrees pizza restaurant next to my apartment makes personalization options seem almost endless. I'd be lying if I said they were all healthy, but even I can find a few good options. At 800 Degrees, you can create your own pie exactly the way you want it. Want a healthy meal? Try a gluten-free crust, a little olive oil, grilled chicken, and lots of veggies. Only want onions on half or even a quarter? No problem. You can even build a reasonable replica of the half quadruple extra cheese, half "Meat Lovers" pizza advertised a million times on basically any sports broadcast. Four people can sit at the same table and have four absolutely, completely different pizza experiences. It just comes down to how they've chosen to personally fill in their pies.

Everyone living on this planet shares two things in common: we each have twenty-four hours available to us every day, and we each have options for how we fill those hours.

I used to think I never had enough time for myself; I felt like there was never enough time to work out or to just sit and relax with loved ones. But that wasn't actually true—I just didn't understand that I controlled my time with my choices. I could walk into the restaurant of life, and either: (1) Refuse to choose my own time toppings, allow the workers (society) to make my pizza for me, and then be disappointed and depressed when I was served a big pie full of garbage, or (2) I could carefully select the exact toppings that I enjoy and love.

If you treat each day like a twenty-four-hour pie that you get to fill, you realize that you have more than enough time to live the way you want—every day. Sure, there will be challenges, road bumps, or things you don't necessarily look forward to, but overall, you can always have enough time for the things you love. You have the choice to fill your days with healthy life-sustaining options or ones that take you further and further away from being the best *you* that you can be.

Let's break down this personal-time pizza:

On average, eight hours of the twenty-four should go toward sleep. You have sixteen left; of those, let's say you work eight.

You now have eight hours left. Throw in an hour of commuting to and from work, an hour for getting ready, and an hour for eating. That leaves five hours left in your day. Any way you look at it, five hours is a lot of time. Those are your completely blank slices! You can choose whatever toppings you want. Just like some pizza toppings complement each other, your life toppings can complement each other too, allowing you to double up. You can't double up on everything (don't try to sleep and practice the violin at the same time, unless you are some sort of Beethoven savant or enjoy being booked into your local jail for disturbing the peace). But mixing cooking dinner with quality family time? That's a winning combo.

When Ted and I looked at his pizza, we realized that by choosing a few healthier options, he could create quite a bit of "extra" time in his average day. The one to two hours he spent watching golf could be cut to ten to twenty minutes for updates and highlights.

Boom, just like that, he created an hour and a half of free time each day. He dedicated some of that new time to helping his wife cook dinner (which she loved, as her love languages are acts of service and quality time). This helped to create a stronger, more enjoyable bond in their marriage. He realized he could "double up" on work commutes by listening to podcasts and audiobooks, learning about a variety of topics he had always wanted to find the time to study. He could set aside one day per week (usually Sunday) for a family adventure—no work, no email, no golf highlights, just time for recharging and bonding with his wife and kids, prioritizing the people who matter most.

Ted chose these four healthy "pizza of life" toppings—just four! —and they made all the difference to him *and* his family. Ted was a new man; he not only had more time in his daily life, it was more meaningful and higher quality time.

And that's the *mindset pivot.* It can be easy to wish that there were just a few more hours in each day, but that's not a solution. If you don't choose and control what you do with the twenty-four hours that you have, what makes you think you'd be any less stressed with twenty-eight? That's like ordering a pizza covered in unhealthy toppings you hate, then being upset it isn't bigger—if you're not enjoying your eight-inch anchovies and pineapple pizza, you're not going to like twelve-inches any better! Take control of your time by taking control of your options, and you'll build better, more productive, more joyful days.

I always used to tell people I was slammed with work: "Sorry, I'm super busy, I can't meet up today," or "Sorry, I'm so busy I don't have the five minutes to talk." To me, being busy equaled being important. Late into the evenings, I would pile on email after email just to convince myself that I was doing something of importance. But what I came to realize through creating my own *ultimate life* time pizza is that, in all honesty, busy is complete BS. This "busy" was just an excuse to get me out of things I didn't want to do.

Then, I heard the rumored last words from one of the richest, most successful people in human history (at least in the eyes of the world), Steve Jobs. Essentially, Steve said that no one has ever laid on their deathbed and wished they did more *busywork* throughout the day, spent more time at the office, and less time away from the ones they loved. That struck a chord in me. I knew I was on the same path as Jobs (minus the iPhone invention, of course).

Time is the most valuable resource we have and the only resource we can never get more of. If we are too busy for the ones we love, are we really living out our *ultimate lives*? Remember this: we are never too busy for the people that mean the most to us. Busy is BS.

SUCCESS

BLUEPRINT ACTION PLAN

1. How are you currently constructing your pizza? Fill out the pie with your average day.

    Do you enjoy it? Does the way you fill your day reflect your desires, goals, and loves?

    With those answers, take the time to fill in your *ideal* time pizza, carefully allocating the time that you want to spend on each area of your life.

    Now, reflect on how this day feels to you, and compare it with your first pizza. What pivots can you make to bring these two pizzas into alignment?

2. Write down "CHOOSE YOUR DAILY PIZZA TOPPINGS" on a notecard and tape it next to the clock you look at most frequently throughout the day. Commit to noting what you've chosen to fill your last slice with and what you're going to fill your next slice with each time you glance at this clock.

AVERAGE

IDEAL

DAY 16

THE 82.5 POUND STONE ON THE BOTTOM OF THE OCEAN

KYLE KORVER IS FROM MY hometown, a tiny cornfield that wouldn't even show up on most maps. He is also, hands down, one of the best shooters in NBA history. But he wasn't "supposed" to be what he is today—he wasn't "supposed" to make it out of Iowa. He wasn't even "supposed" to play basketball at all.

When I attended basketball camp in high school, the director used Kyle's story as an example. No one *gave* Kyle any sort of advantage or special treatment, and he wasn't so incredibly gifted with natural athletic talent that professional basketball was his inevitable future. In fact, he almost didn't play college ball—he didn't have a single scholarship offer to his name until Creighton University decided to give him one at the twenty-fifth hour. But the rest is history—college to NBA to NBA super stardom. He was even a final candidate for the USA Olympic Basketball team in 2016. That's basically saying he was one of the top twenty players in the world!

So, how does someone who isn't "gifted" go on to accomplish all that Kyle has?

After an off-season workout, I was sitting with Kyle outside of the Santa Barbara Whole Foods, finishing the last few slurps of a smoothie that tasted way too good to be that green. We'd been talking about the good old days in Pella, Iowa, sharing stories of the high school coach we'd both had, and reminiscing about Dutch Letters pastries (which might actually be the best tasting thing known to man).

As we soaked in the summer sun and laughed at the stories and the interesting journeys we'd both taken to get to where we were, I asked Kyle, "What drove you every day?"

I was expecting some version of the same shallow answer most professional athletes give— "I want to be the best, so I train as if I'm the best." But he paused for a second, finding the right words to express exactly what he wanted to say. It was worth the wait, because I will never forget his response—words I live by to this day:

"David, I've been given a gift to shoot a basketball. A talent God gave me to use. If I don't maximize that talent, what good does it do? Why was I even given the talent in the first place? There are people out there who could care less about basketball. But what if they can learn how to love others because I was able to reach them through this talent? I wanted to make my talent have purpose."

I was blown away. Kyle didn't view his gift of shooting a basketball in terms of basketball at all—he saw it as a vehicle for so much more. That's why and how he pushes himself to grow daily—on the court, off the court, as a father, as a husband, as an overall person. He pushes himself like he has never played a single minute in the NBA, because the NBA was never the *only* goal. He pushes himself like he has a secret gift to give everyone throughout the world, and the only way to get it out there is to maximize his own drive.

Kyle realizes basketball is just his vehicle to help others.

Every year, Kyle does something to push his limits, knowing that, no matter the success the world has told him he has achieved, he has developed his gift into a platform to share so much more. Every off-season, he reminds himself of how he got to where he is today by doing something so physically and mentally challenging that it absolutely embodies the mindset pivot of *thriving over surviving.*

Okay, so, if most of us were to consider tackling physical challenges outside our daily comfort zones, we might think about bungee jumping, or marathon running, or, if we're getting really adventurous, skydiving.

Not Kyle. He's different. And maybe even a little crazy. Like, "pushing an 82.5-pound stone on the bottom of the ocean floor for hours through shark-infested waters" crazy.

No, I didn't make that up. That's exactly what Kyle did one summer day in the chilly waters off the pristine coast of Santa Cruz Island. Fourteen laps, underwater, pushing through sand that might as well have been cement, with less-than-optimal oxygen intake and a very real awareness that if he gave into exhaustion that far underwater, the probability of coming up alive was low. Oh, and the bonus possibility that one of the great white sharks who were never more than ten feet away would decide his arm was a good lunchtime nibble.

Who in their right mind comes out of this self-created living-hell obstacle course grinning from ear-to-ear?

Kyle.

This man not only *survives,* he *thrives.*

Now, I definitely understand that the eighty-two-game NBA

season is an absolute grind. It's tough on a player's body, and every committed athlete has to put in some painful work to build up strength in the off-season if they want to thrive on the court. But there has to be an easier—and more effective—way than Kyle's techniques to get in basketball-shooting-shape, right?

Maybe for the body, but Kyle has found a surefire way to train his mind—to pivot from being comfortable and just *surviving* day-to-day to embracing the uncomfortable and *thriving* every day. Sure, it might be a little extreme, but you can't argue with the results. He's combined the motivation of knowing his true purpose with the training he needs to build a healthy body and superhuman mental strength. You definitely don't get that just from shooting practice free-throws.

We do what we need to do to survive, at least the majority of the time. We keep ourselves physically strong enough to keep our heads above water. We breathe, we eat, we sleep—even if we're not doing any of it optimally, we do it. But just like we tend to neglect our physical needs when we're struggling, we neglect building our mental strength as well. Think about it. Do you wake up every morning worried about how you are going to get through the day ahead? Do you anxiously watch the clock, waiting to check out of the office, only to get into a car that is due for an inspection you don't know if you can afford and go home to young kids who could care less about your depleted energy and a house that needs to be cleaned? Do you fear how you are going to survive this day—day after day after day?

Believe it or not, that fear, that survival-mode, keeps you in a spot where you can never possibly do anything *but* survive. Survival mode locks you out of thriving mode, and the key that pivots you back and forth between the two doesn't even exist. It doesn't matter if you manage to get the car inspected, the house cleaned, and the kids in bed. You'll still live in fear of that next thing, the next day, and the millions of other things you need to tackle. Life becomes a constant uphill climb, and you just barely eke out the strength to make it through. We've all been there, we've all had that feeling.

But it can all be changed. We don't have to feel like this or live in constant daily survival mode. It's all about pivoting the mindset from *surviving* to *thriving*. Waking up each morning and understanding the day ahead is an opportunity to *thrive*. Going to work and positively encouraging someone, empowering a co-worker to reach new limits they never thought they could hit. Swallowing the car inspection cost because you know your bank account isn't what gives you joy and stability—it's the safety of the family at home, the kids waiting for you to scoop them up for hugs the moment you walk in the door. It's the ability to live each day with the full-plate mentality: knowing that God is going to fill your plate up with only the things you will get done in that one day, giving you the comfort and contentment of knowing you did all you could for the day with the plate you were given and that your plate will be filled again tomorrow. It's a full-plate mentality that allows us to shut off the *surviving* worries and turn on the *thriving* power. It's not an endless buffet mentality, where we suffocate ourselves.

My favorite Bible verse is Mathew 6:26-27: "Look at the birds of the air; they do not sow or reap or store away in barns, and yet your heavenly Father feeds them. Are you not much more valuable than they? Can any one of you by worrying add a single hour to your life?"

We are all going to have struggles throughout our lives. More than likely, we are going to have struggles daily. It's just how life is. However, the confidence we gain by going through these challenging times, knowing we will make it through no matter what gets thrown our way (even if it's an 82.5 pound boulder) makes everything in life better. We come out the other side stronger, with an even deeper knowledge of our true selves.

That's exactly why Kyle walks the ocean floors, pushing boulders, weaving in and out of great white sharks. Not only for his own personal self-growth, but to use his platform to show others that we can *thrive* in any situation, even in the darkest *survival* modes. That's why he is driven to extreme measures to use his God-given gifts. That's why Kyle changed his mindset from *surviving* to *thriving*.

Now, the question is, will you?

BLUEPRINT ACTION PLAN

1. Inside the shark, write down one thing that makes you feel like you are "underwater" this week, whether it is a bill you need to pay, an errand you need to run, or a phone call you need to return.

   Now, fill in the boat with how you'll defeat this shark—not through sheer pushing through, but while *thriving*. How can you turn this into a positive experience? Perhaps you can pay the bills while watching a movie with your kids—or better yet, while teaching your kids how to pay bills and where money comes from! That's thriving, that's taking a dreaded obligation and making it meaningful in your life and helpful for others. Take a break from another problem you're trying to solve to go for a walk and return a phone call from a family member; talk about one great memory you have together. That's thriving—you'll not only make the day for someone you love, you'll clear your head and have much better results when you focus back on your challenge.

2. Write down "THRIVING OVER SURVIVING" on a notecard and tape it above your toilet. Whenever you are using the bathroom, take a moment to appreciate that you're not swirling underwater— you are up above, thriving.

DAY 17
CHAMPIONSHIP SOUVLAKIS

BACK WHEN I WAS PLAYING in Athens, Greece, I had an Aussie teammate named Aron who was 7' tall and 260 pounds of rock-solid muscle. I liked Aron as a person and I knew he was a good player, but I didn't necessarily have a whole lot of respect for his attitude or work ethic right off the bat. Don't get me wrong, he would work hard—he was in the gym early and he stayed late to lift weights—he just never really acted like he wanted to be there. I took a little offense to this, since, at 6'2" and unable to dunk in a sport that thrives on athleticism, I had to scratch tooth and nail to get anything in the basketball world. I was playing for peanuts (or, more accurately, souvlakis and tzatziki dip), and this dude just didn't seem to appreciate how good he could actually be.

The season ended and our team was far from making the play-offs, which I was actually pretty excited about—that meant I got to go back to the United States early! (There's no better feeling than stepping off the airplane back home after being gone for months on end.) Throughout our time together in Greece, Aron and I had bonded over our love for the best souvlaki restaurant in town, Thanasis Souvlaki, so it only seemed right to go one last time before we went our separate ways.

We sat outside in the May sunshine with the rest of the population of Athens. (It's an amazing spectacle to see, actually. If the sun is out, not a single soul works—everyone sits at cafes and drinks espresso.) Aron and I ordered a meal that would easily have fed a large family that hadn't eaten in a week.

I knew this was probably the last time I would ever see Aron, so, inhaling food, I asked, "How come you disliked being here?"

The question didn't throw him off his game. In between bites, he responded, "I didn't, mate. I liked it."

"Then why didn't it look like it?"

Now, that one surprised him. He placed his souvlaki down on his plate and finished chewing his mouthful slowly. "I looked like I don't like it?"

For thirty minutes, we went back and forth about different situations that had given me the impression that Aron was not giving everything he had, that he would rather be anywhere else, or that he just didn't really care. Eventually, we came to the conclusion that Aron perceived himself as being better than the team he was on, and better than the situation he was given. He thought he should be playing at a higher level (which, in all honesty, he definitely should have). The truth of the matter was, though, that Aron wasn't going to go to a higher level if he kept *going through the motions* with an attitude that didn't portray his true talent.

As we split the bill (basically the last of the euros I had earned the entire season), Aron gave me a hug and said, "Thank you for being a friend and caring about me, mate. It means a lot."

Aron played another season in Europe with Partizan, a team in Belgrade, Serbia, a small step up from the situation in Greece. I, of course, played half a season in Spain. We would shoot each other a text here and there, checking in and debating whose country had the best food (nothing came close to competing with Thanasis Souvlaki, that's for sure!). When I was sent home from Spain, though, our communication slowly tapered off.

By the time I'd made it to Oakland and my friend Kris's guest room, it'd been about four months since Aron and I had last talked. Sitting on the couch watching NBA games on a Saturday afternoon, Kris and I just so happened to change the channel to the San Antonio Spurs game. And there was Aron, in a Spurs uniform with "Baynes" stitched across the back, waving his towel on the bench with more passion and excitement than I had ever seen in anyone.

I was stunned, excited, and very confused. I rapidly texted everyone I knew, including Aron mid-game, congratulating him and letting him know how proud I was. My former teammate was playing for the best team in the NBA.

Aron texted me back after the game was over: "Thanks, mate, great to hear from you. I'm going to be the best towel waver you've ever seen this year!"

All I could do was smile. No matter the situation, I knew Aron was going to give his absolute best.

Since that day, we talk all the time. We visit each other when we are in the same city, send food pictures back and forth constantly, and reminisce about the old days in Greece often. I consider him one of my best friends; he was one of my groomsmen in my wedding. And he kept true to his word. If you follow the NBA, you probably know Aron Baynes as the rough, tough, blue collar Aussie big man.

Aron has had a very successful career, winning a championship with the San Antonio Spurs, playing for the Boston Celtics, and earning well over $50 million. Funny what just a simple mindset pivot can do for your perspective and overall trajectory of life.

It just goes to show you that no one is bigger than the situations they find themselves in. If you don't embrace your circumstances with everything you've got, you will never reach the next step towards where you want to be. If you are cleaning windows at a carwash, be the best window scrubber there is. Do everything with the best of your ability, knowing that bigger and better things will come your way as long as you *wave your towel.*

Take a second to think about the job you have right now and the spot you are at in your career. You've come a long way. When you really stop and reflect, you'll remember that you have battled through a lot. Think about all the small details that had to line up exactly in your favor—more than any of us can ever even know, much less control. We are not defined by our current situations.

NBA players are perceived as superheroes—we call Shaq "Superman," Dwayne Wade "Batman," and attribute basically every superhero power combined to LeBron James (which might actually be true). But the truth of the matter is, they are only human. They have incredible gifts they constantly work to develop, but they fear failure and lose confidence just like us. It's tough to believe that players at the highest level of their sport would doubt their abilities, but it's absolutely true.

When I was coaching with the Brooklyn Nets, we called up a player, Sean Kilpatrick, from the NBA D-League (basically the

PASSION

minor league system of the NBA). He had already done a couple stints in the NBA, but to no avail.

I met Sean for the first time when he stepped on the team bus during a road trip in Los Angeles. He looked me in the eyes, weary and desperate, and said, "Coach, I'll do anything it takes to make it. I know this is my last shot."

I could tell his hunger was genuine. I knew he had a young daughter to provide for. I told him he would make the team.

Now, I honestly had no idea if he would or wouldn't; that was out of my control, in God's hands. But I could see his fears and anxieties; he hadn't made it yet, and he didn't know whether he could believe in himself anymore. He needed a teammate, waving the towel, to boost his confidence.

We were playing the Lakers the next day, so there wasn't a lot that I could do to help Sean improve his basketball skill set overnight. He would wake up as the same player with the same shot. The only thing we could work on, the only way to give him a chance at the NBA—his last chance—was to pivot his mindset.

Sean and I started going through a ton of his old film from Cincinnati University, where he'd been the second all-time leading scorer. On those tapes, Sean was very talented, an extremely dynamic scorer. But mentally, he was stuck with what he'd accomplished during his last stint in the NBA, with the Denver Nuggets . . . nothing.

We talked deep into the night about his most enjoyable times on the basketball court growing up. Sean took me back to his days in White Plains, New York, where he walked on to the local playground and everyone knew who he was. Where he stepped onto his high school basketball court and evoked fear in his opponents' eyes. Where he was "the man"—he had actually been given the keys to the city, which designated a Sean Kilpatrick Day. He had a whole town of towel wavers, but they certainly weren't going to be in LA the next day for his game against the Lakers.

The next evening, Sean and I sat quietly together in the locker room an hour before tipoff. He had just finished his shooting routine on court and was physically warmed up. Now, it was time to really get him ready to go.

"Hey, Sean, where are we right now?"

He looked like he was a little concerned for me. "Staples Center, coach."

"Wrong answer, that's where every one of those Lakers players are. Where are *we*?"

He looked very confused for a moment, and then a huge smile spread across his face. With a confident swag, he said, "We in White Plains, we definitely in White Plains."

I knew from that moment that he was locked in.

Sean didn't play in the first quarter of the game, but he looked over to me in the huddle and winked, mouthing, "We got this, coach." He knew I was there to wave the towel for him, and he was waving it right back at me. Mentally, we were on the blacktop court in White Plains.

When Sean checked into the game in the second quarter, he came out guns blazing. Offensively, he brought a level of dynamic

PASSION

energy that the Nets desperately needed; defensively, he smothered his match-up and communicated like a man possessed.

This level of confidence coming from a ten-day D-League call-up player spread like a plague to the rest of his Nets team-mates. He changed the game—he brought us *all* to White Plains. Even though D'Angelo Russell went off that night to eventually lead the Lakers to a win, Sean's impact on the energy and flow of the game was very noticeable and the talk of the Brooklyn coaches and management. By the time the final buzzer went off, we were all waving the towel for Sean.

Sean came to me directly after the game, gave me a big hug, and said, "Coach, we here to stay. This league is going to know about White Plains."

Sean went on to sign a contract with the Nets for the remainder of the season and a three-year contract extension afterwards. He was no longer an NBA hopeful; he was an NBA player, a contributor. He even became a starter the following season. Sean was a true towel-waving superhero.

If you think about it, Sean and Aron were both struggling with the same problem: they couldn't fully be there for their teammates because mentally, they were so caught up worrying about their own less-than-optimal situations. Neither of them could make it to the next level until they made the most of the present moment—until they not only brought in their swag, but also built a team of towel wavers by leading the towel-waving themselves. Basketball, like life, isn't a one-man sport—none of us are self-made, we all need the help of those around us. If we breathe self-confidence and encouragement into others, it creates a domino effect. John Maxwell, an inspiration and role model of mine, sums it all up as: *"One is too small a number to achieve greatness."* You cannot do anything of *real* value alone.

You're always in training, and, just like you didn't make it where you currently are by yourself, you won't make it to the next level alone either. So, stand up and wave your towel as hard as you can, every single day, because your call-up is right around the corner.

PASSION

BLUEPRINT ACTION PLAN

1. On the towel, write down three ways that you can be a better teammate. It could be listening to your co-worker who is going through a rough patch in their marriage, it could be helping your daughter each night with her math homework, or it could be as simple as patting everyone at work on the back and positively encouraging them. Commit to doing those three things every day this week, and remind yourself that you're not just building your strength as a person—you're building the strength of your whole team!

2. Write down "I STAND AND WAVE MY TOWEL" on a notecard and tape it wherever you keep your towels. Commit to reflect on the ways you have and can cheer people on today whenever you pass it.

DAY 18
MULTI-MILLIONAIRE MINION

IMAGINE AN NBA AGENT WHO reps multiple max contract players, juggling their shoe deals and movie options from a private jet flying all over the world. He sits front row at any NBA game, a true power player, basically a living, breathing version of Jerry Maguire. Impressive, right? My friend, who (to respect his personal privacy) we'll call Jerry, was that guy. He was at the very top of an exceptionally difficult, *very* lucrative career, and no one in the business did it better.

One early October afternoon during the NBA pre-season, Jerry and I were sitting in his office, joking and talking about how his players were in great spots. They were thankful for their contracts and thankful for the royal treatment they had received in the off season—but we both knew that peace and serenity could all come crashing down in an instant with any small issue. That's the life of an agent: putting out constant fires. We joked about how Jerry would be happier if he went completely *Office Space* (a movie you definitely need to see if you haven't), quit caring what anyone thought of him, and started saying "no" to everything. Literally everything.

"Can I get a max deal contract?"
"No."

"Can I be in a movie?"

"No."

I could tell the wheels were turning in Jerry's head; he was having a great time talking about it and imagining what it would actually be like to live this life. But nothing would come of it. After all, Jerry was one of the most powerful NBA agents. He had to be happy, right?

Well, not exactly. Little did I know, Jerry was actually pretty miserable.

He called me two weeks later and immediately broke down. "David, I have to say no. I can't keep saying yes to everything my players and these NBA teams and the other agents ask of me. It's driving me insane. I can't take it anymore. I'm going to have a heart attack and lose my family if I keep this up."

Whoa. I definitely hadn't been expecting that, especially since Jerry always seemed so fun-loving, light-hearted, and heavily sarcastic. But this was far from humorous.

He went on to tell me that he had been wearing a mask. He wasn't doing what he wanted to do, but what others wanted of him. He couldn't say no; he had set the expectation that he'd say yes to every request. His peers, his players, everyone who knew him would say things like, "You can always count on Jerry to do what is asked." That's the label Jerry carried around with him. And it had gotten him to this point, to the very top of the power chain.

"Jerry—if you lost it all, would you be able to live with yourself and support your family financially?"

He said he would. He had earned and saved enough money that he could live comfortably for a while; he would probably be at much greater peace, in much better mental and physical health, and most importantly, a much better father and husband to his family.

He talked for a while about how he'd never really wanted to be an agent in the first place; that was never his passion and never really what he'd felt called to do. He wanted to help others; he wanted to feel like he was contributing to society. Jerry's real passion was philanthropy: being hands-on while giving back to the less fortunate. He told me that he felt most alive when he was giving to others and making others smile. Not when he was rubbing elbows with the elite of the elite in NBA circles.

I applauded him for coming to that conclusion. That was step one. Now, it was time to take step two . . .

And order a Minion character statue, of course.

Yes, a Minion, from the *Despicable Me* franchise. The little yellow guys that are basically glorified robotic "yes men" and do anything anyone tells them to do. Jerry needed to put one on his desk. Why? That way, every day, he would see that Minion, and it would remind him that he could and needed to SAY NO!

"Jerry, there are going to be a lot of really good options and opportunities that come your way, as there already have been. There are going to be current NBA players who want to work with you, future high draft picks who want to sign with you, shoe deals, movie deals, record labels—you name it. But you have to say no. If you say yes, you will be right back on the hamster wheel and you will never get off. You will surprise people by saying no, you will upset people by saying no, you will lose money (opportunity-cost money that is, which is *not the same as real money-in-hand money*), but you will find the sense of joy and peace that you desperately need."

It would not be easy, but it had sunk in. Jerry changed that evening. He took real action steps. He set a financial target; when he reached it, his family would be secure even if he never worked again. He put an automated response on his phone and email for any message that he received: "I'm currently in 'no meeting mode,' as I need to put my head down and focus on the work directly at hand." (A GREAT line, if I do say so myself. It lets people know you are unavailable, but you will get back to them on your time; it also makes you sound as if you are locked in on a very important project. I actually used this very same line while I wrote this book. There were many distractions that could have put off the daily writing, but I was 'locked in on an important project.')

Jerry brought on an understudy so that he could slowly start handing off his current clients. During that new "free time" he created, he began to volunteer at the local chapter of his church's non-profit. He said "no" to every outlandish request a player made; he would straight up tell them it was not realistic. If that wasn't what they wanted to hear, they could go to another agency; Jerry knew it couldn't possibly be delivered and it would never materialize for them.

To Jerry's surprise, he didn't lose a single client. He actually gained more respect from his players and his peers. People now viewed Jerry's time as much more valuable, and he was considered completely truthful (something very rare in the agent business). Jerry had done it: he'd mastered the art of saying no. And not only

SUCCESS

did he not lose everything, his business thrived and could have continued to thrive, had he actually been passionate about it.

I don't see much of Jerry anymore, but I know he is at peace with his life. I still get texts from time to time. Most of the time, it is a picture of the Minion, who now lives on his kitchen table, a humorous (but still important) reminder to Jerry that he has the power to say no.

Jerry has been out of the agency business for a few years now. At what some considered to be the pinnacle of his career, Jerry handed all of his clients to his understudy and walked away with peace, joy, and a sense of great accomplishment in his newfound ability to say no. He now consults for multiple non-profits, but only part time. He is a full-time loving father and husband. He gave up on potential millions, walked away from a life that (on the surface) was extremely enviable, and turned his back on what society thought he should do and who he'd been told he was. Jerry mastered the art of saying no, and in doing so, he mastered the art of fully living his life.

We've all heard about how important it is to get rid of the trivial "lots" to focus on the select few important things in life. But it's so much easier said than actually done. Everyone has an innate drive to please others, and with that desire comes far too many *yeses*.

Think about it: how often do you say yes to something right away and immediately regret it? It happens all the time. Way more than you would probably like to admit. That's because most of us don't fully understand the art of saying no. But once you realize that saying no is a part of your superhero power of *choice*, you will find your joy and peace and become your true self, the person who you were fully made to be.

BLUEPRINT ACTION PLAN

1. Inside the three statement bubbles below, write down three things you've said "yes" to in the recent past (or some that you routinely say "yes" to) that you regretted.

In the opposing thought bubbles, write down the things you wish you'd spent your time, energy, and passion saying "yes" to instead.

Remember this exercise the next time you get ready to say "yes" to something that you'd be in much better shape saying "no" to—that "yes" might make someone happier in the moment, but who and what is it taking you away from?

2. Write down "MY 'NO' MAKES MY 'YES' EVEN STRONGER" on a notecard and tape it to your TV remote control. Commit to reflecting on the choices you get to say "yes" and "no" to each time you turn on your TV.

DAY 19
LISTEN TO THE LYRICS

HOPPING IN THE PASSENGER'S SEAT of Jeremy Lin's car, I was caught off guard by his music: Justin Bieber. Let's just say the Biebs isn't my first choice, and I was surprised it would be his. And it didn't seem to be a mistake—Jeremy was rocking out.

"So . . .?" I asked, pointing to the radio.

Jeremy smiled. "Man, I can relate. That's me. Listen to the lyrics, they speak directly to me."

And he was right. Justin Bieber had shot straight to the top of world fame; it got the best of him. His songs echoed getting caught up in the lifestyle and succumbing to what others thought of him and the expectations the world placed on him. The album Jeremy was pumping through his multi-leveled car speakers was Bieber's cry for help to find joy and peace.

I didn't know Jeremy during the height of the Lin-Sanity phenomenon (which made the front page of every newspaper, was the main story on every news and sports station, and trended for weeks as the number one story in the world. Yeah, that's not a typo, the WORLD!). I certainly knew about it—I can't imagine the size of the rock you'd have to live under to have missed it. We've talked a lot about it in hindsight. As thankful and grateful as Jeremy was for it all, he would NEVER want to go through it again. Directly after Lin-Sanity, he wrestled with constant *what ifs*: What if I don't perform like this again? What if I can't keep this up? What will people think of me? With the lights and cameras always on him, he wasn't able to enjoy the moment; he was always worried about what was coming next.

The world's expectations can play games with your mind. Fame and notoriety, seeing yourself on TV and magazine covers, being one of the top news stories—all of this can affect a person in ways we'd never imagine. Most of us won't experience it at the level Jeremy did (and that's probably for the better!), but we can all relate to how burdensome the expectations and opinions of others can be.

Jeremy is one of my closest friends and I have been blessed to watch him develop into the person he is today—one of the most genuine, joyful, confident-in-his-own skin guys I have ever met. I've been with Jeremy when he has invited homeless people off the streets of San Francisco to dinner and then listened intently for hours to their life stories. I've been with him when he's been swarmed in public by hundreds of fans, all asking for pictures and autographs, and watched him give out every single one with a genuine smile on his face. And I was there on the night when our waiter just so happened to be Asian with a half-shaved/half-dreadlocked hairstyle, which inspired Jeremy; he grew out the same exact hairstyle to show everyone that the world's judgments don't hold any power over our pure daily joy, passion for living, or confidence in who we are. Jeremy freed himself of the expectations the world had placed upon him.

What was your favorite class in elementary school? Don't tell me it was science or math; I know it wasn't (unless you're a nerd like my wife). It was recess! We all woke up excited about what we were going to play with our friends, what adventures we could create on the monkey bars, and how many times we could run up the slide and slide down without falling off. Recess was the best class by far, but why?

We were free. There was no one telling us that we had to be great at this or that. There were no grades, there were no perfect test scores, there were no report cards to bring home to show our production level or personal growth, and there weren't any expectations that we had to live up to. At recess, we could play, we could imagine, we could escape our identities and allow ourselves to be bad at something if we wanted to try it out. We had the freedom to explore what we loved to do and figure out what made us who we truly were.

Another good friend of mine is NBA superstar Brook Lopez. Brook is one of the best true NBA big men to play in the past twenty years, during a time when the big man has gone the way of the dinosaurs—from plentiful and dominant to nearly extinct. Brook transcended that shift. But trust me, it wasn't easy.

Brook is a very gifted and extremely talented basketball player with athletic abilities and hand-eye coordination that don't even make sense for a 7' man to possess. He came into the NBA from Stanford as a "can't miss" prospect, a future multiple All-Star, someone to build a franchise around, a potential Hall of Famer. Brook was that good and in a league that desperately needed great big men. As the tenth pick overall in the 2008 draft, Brook landed in New Jersey, on a team that needed a high IQ big man as a savior.

But as good as Brook was on the court, the New Jersey Nets

still struggled badly. They not only missed the playoffs in his first season, but they accumulated one of the worst records in NBA history (12-70) in his second. Brook showed consistency and flashes of greatness, but never lived up to the expectations. He was only an All-Star one time, in 2013, and barely ever experienced the taste of the playoffs. And it killed him; he heard what everyone was saying, he saw their disappointment. He was an emotional guy, and there was no way for him to stop caring about what others thought.

Led by the brilliance of a young Steph Curry and the Golden State Warriors, the NBA evolved into a guard-dominated league, and the need for a true big man was gone. Former $100-million contract players, gone. Vanished. Brook had to adapt and transition or he would suffer the same fate as the big man dinosaurs before him.

I arrived to the team after the New Jersey Nets moved over to Brooklyn. I knew Brook by his reputation, as a basketball player who had never lived up to super high expectations. There had also been some stories that Brook and his twin brother Robin (also an NBA player) were a little different—something that was inevitably painted in a negative light. As Brook and I got closer and he began to trust me, I realized that playing basketball might have made the fifth or sixth slot on his lists of interests, no way defining him.

We were in Orlando, getting destroyed by the Magic, and Brook was taking all of the wrath of the coach. I could tell he wasn't fully into the game; he was not his normal, dominant self on the court. We got back to the hotel after being absolutely obliterated, and I went off to bed. I was physically and emotionally drained from the game, plus, I'm a morning person; I like to be up and going at the crack of dawn.

Awaiting me at the crack of dawn, though, was a text from Brook: "Do you want to go to Epcot?" When I got down to the lobby at 6:59 AM, halfway through my cup of coffee and still struggling to fully wake up, Brook greeted me with a smile as wide as he was tall, ready to take on Disneyworld.

As we ran around the park for nearly three hours that morning, going on ride after ride before we had to hightail it back to the hotel to catch the team meeting, I saw something in Brook that I hadn't seen before: genuine joy. This was where Brook could be himself, not on the basketball court. Here, he was comfortable in his own skin, without worrying about living up to any expectations. Brook was at peace; he was in his happy place.

As the season progressed, the fate of the Nets didn't improve. But Brook? Brook thrived. It didn't show up in wins and losses; it showed up in the person he was on the floor and the teammate he was in the locker room, slowly shedding the impenetrable shield that he had built around himself. Brook was not only being true to himself; he was being true to his skill set. He began realizing what it was going to take to transition into the "new" NBA, the three-point shooting-obsessed NBA, which required even seven footers, previously planted around the rim, to step twenty-three feet back and consistently knock down shots. Brook fully embraced it. Over the next three seasons, he was not only one of the top three point shooters out of the big men in the NBA, he was a top three point shooter in ALL of the NBA. Brook even went on to break the NBA record for three pointers made by a player 7' or taller.

Brook didn't just survive; he thrived. He found himself that day at Epcot. He found that he could be who he was, comfortable in his own skin. He found that he could accept his goofy, fun-loving self. He found that he could even bring his Star Wars action figures into the locker room and no one would condemn him. Brook wasn't defined by the stereotypical assumptions of how a basketball player should be, and he found definition to his own life.

Late in that season, while facing the LA Lakers during Kobe Bryant's farewell tour, instead of seeking out Kobe for an autographed jersey like every other player, Brook sat in the corner of the locker room and spoke with an unassuming old Japanese lady for thirty minutes. She was a reporter for an anime magazine, another one of Brook's interests and loves. As I watched the Kobe-mania on one side and Brook locked-in on the other, talking about Japanese cartoons, I could only sit back and smile. Brook was no longer burdened with hiding who he truly was; he could freely be himself.

When you meet someone, how often do you ask them what they do right off the bat? And how often do you immediately judge someone based on their answer? How often do you tell someone what you do before they know anything else about you? Is that truly your identity? As a society, we get so caught up with our image and the need to impress those around us that it ends up engulfing who we truly are. It's like letting the evil version of ourselves take charge of our bodies while our minds are trapped, screaming to escape. Free yourself from those chains; let those burdens go. Allow yourself to be just okay or even bad at something. Allow yourself to play again. Allow yourself to be back on the recess blacktop, running around with your friends, searching for a lost treasure. Free yourself from the self-created identity you think you have to live up to. Choose to be fully YOU. It's a mindset pivot—*imagination over identity*—that will bring you joy, peace, and the ability to truly succeed as the person you were meant to be.

BLUEPRINT ACTION PLAN

1. Fill in the closet with the "quirky" things about you that make you different from everyone else—things that you might not want everyone to know, that you've tried to keep under wraps.

For me, I would have to include my Ugg boots. They just put me in a super comfy, peaceful state of mind. Since I'm a go-getter, someone who builds my career on keeping energy high and never slacking, these shoes don't send out the same message, so for a long time, I kept them a little hidden. Yes, the shame—I like warm, comfortable footwear. Sounds silly now, but it was honestly not something I necessarily wanted everyone knowing. Once I realized that bringing that sense of comfort and peace into my wardrobe only helped me be more myself, I started embracing it and wearing them in public. You wouldn't believe the compliments I get on them! Embracing all of me, even the parts that don't make sense against the stereotypes, makes everything I commit myself to stronger—trust me, it's going to work for you too!

After you've filled your own closet, write down what you like about your hidden pleasure and why you've been afraid to show that side of yourself to the world. Commit to wearing yours out somewhere today!

2. Write down "I AM FREE TO BE ME!" on a notecard and tape it to your closet door. Commit to reflecting on the portions of yourself you try to hide from judgment and what steps you're taking to share them with the world each time you open your closet.

DAY 20
BOARD GAME CHANGER

WHAT IS THE ONE GREATEST thing you can do for a stranger? Is it to give them food, give them money, say hello and smile? Most people will accept kindness in the moment, but if you really care about making an impact on lives, help and encourage people to follow their passions—that is the greatest, longest lasting gift you can give.

My close friend Jeremy Lin (NBA superstar and Bieber fan) was doing a year of rehab in Vancouver, British Columbia, for the knee injury he had sustained during the very first game of the season. One wet, very cold winter night while our good friend Arron and I were visiting him, the three of us dominated four escape rooms in a row, then celebrated our record-setting feats by demolishing food at a Thai restaurant. We followed that up with the obvious choice to keep this party going—a riveting board game.

Our board game battle the previous night had left Jeremy bragging about his "hidden talent" (which was just getting super lucky, if you ask me). We needed something new, a game of real skill and strategy, so that Arron and I could redeem ourselves.

As fate would have it, we spotted a small storefront completely dedicated to board games just a block away from the restaurant. Crazy odds, right? I hadn't even known stores like this existed.

Well, it wouldn't for much longer—walking in, we noticed a sign that read, "Going out of business, one week left."

Inside, I could see why it was going under: this store was dedicated to the childhood dreams and obsessions of the owner. These games were not the Monopoly types we all grew up playing, but games you have never heard of before. Or, at least, I hadn't. Jeremy was like a ten-year-old at Disney World, darting from game to game and strategizing (while talking tons of trash, of course) about how he would annihilate Arron and me at any of them.

While the store owner rang up four games for us, Jeremy told him this was his new favorite store in Vancouver and expressed regret that he hadn't known about it sooner. He asked why they were going out of business. The owner responded, "I love board games, and I wanted to share that love with the world, but no one else seems to want it."

I got lost reading the incredibly intricate directions on the back of one of the games (maybe we shouldn't have let Jeremy choose, and maybe his winning streak wasn't solely luck-based after all) while Jeremy and the owner kept chatting. I noticed the growing excitement in the owner's voice and eyes, so I figured he was asking Jeremy questions about playing in the NBA. I tuned back into the conversation once I noticed the owner was shining brighter than the Christmas lights strung up outside. As I listened more closely, I realized that this guy wasn't a basketball fan; in fact, he didn't even know who Jeremy was. He was all lit up because Jeremy was telling his story of following his passion when the rest of the world said it couldn't be done and no one believed in him.

They must have talked for nearly forty-five minutes that night. Normally, I don't have much patience to stand and wait, but in those forty-five minutes, I realized something. I realized that the best gift you can ever give someone is speaking the life of encouragement into their passion. Jeremy gave the board game store owner hope when he thought no one else appreciated his passion. All it took was one person to change this man's life.

The store did not close down a week later; instead, the owner began to publicize its resurgence. He marketed it throughout Vancouver business newspapers and social media (with Jeremy's help, of course) so thoroughly that it even popped up in advertisements on my phone from time to time once I was back home in Los Angeles.

When I came back later in the year to visit Jeremy, we walked to the board game store after another delicious Thai food dinner and multiple escape-room dominations. The place was swarming with customers this time; nearly twenty-five people squeezed into this nook, all looking for board games. Not only was the store revived and thriving, the board game market in Vancouver was ignited; people had remembered their childhood loves. The smile on my face warmed my insides up (despite the very frigid Vancouver weather)—and then I saw the smile on the owner's face. No words needed to be spoken: To live out one's passion is to live out one's purpose. And all it took was Jeremy speaking life and encouragement into this man's passion for board games.

Can you make a real, substantial difference in someone else's life? Can you tell the pharmacists at your local drug store what a great job they are doing and how much you love the attention to detail they put into every order and every customer? Can you pause as you pass by the construction site on your daily commute, roll down the window, and give the workers a big thumbs-up telling them how beautiful the structure looks and how great they are at what they do? All it takes is a genuine word of encouragement voicing love and admiration for people pursuing their passions. It can make all the difference in their days; it can make all the difference in their lives. It's a mindset pivot—worry less about what others are giving you, and concern yourself with speaking life into others. When you empower people and help them grow their dreams, you will gain more than you can even imagine. Speak life into others, and life will be spoken unto you.

PASSION

BLUEPRINT ACTION PLAN

1. On each of the three domino pieces, write down one person who you really want to empower this month. It could be anyone throughout your day; pay attention to the people you encounter that most people seem to take for granted, and listen closely when people start to share their stories.

After you encourage your chosen person, in the open space below the domino, write down what you did and how it made you feel. Make this a monthly habit for a year, and pay attention to the thirty-six people you've helped empower and how they flourish.

For example, in one of my domino pieces, I've written in the name of my good friend, NBA player Ray McCullum. He wanted to start a podcast and didn't know how to go about it. I knew it would take a lot of time, multiple calls and in-person meetings to set it up for him. I also knew how much he wanted it and how impactful his podcast would be to others. Plus, it was something that he might end up doing full time (broadcasting) when he was done playing. It was something I could empower Ray in that would in turn empower many others. So, even though the time allocation to help him set it up was daunting, I knew it was for a great purpose. Now I get to sit back and listen to each and every podcast, knowing I did my small part to empower this dream!

2. Write down "SPEAK LIFE INTO OTHERS AND I WILL BE FILLED" on a notecard and tape it to the kitchen cabinet that contains your drinking glasses. Commit to reflect on what you are doing to fill others each time you fill a glass.

DAY 21
CHECK THIS OFF!

EVERY TIME TED AND I met for coffee, I could count on having two basic conversations.

Conversation #1: Ted would tell me about the 1964 Shelby Cobra he always dreamed of restoring with his son.

Conversation #2: Ted would tell me he wanted to tackle a book a week, starting with Victor Frankl's *Man's Search for Meaning*.

One Sunday, over my usual giant, steaming hot Americano with a pinch of cinnamon and Ted's go-to vanilla latte with extra pumps of vanilla, I geared up for another round of the same conversation.

"Is the car done yet, Ted? How's the book?"

See, it had been about six months of the same dialogue, to the point where it was a running joke between us. We both knew that he hadn't even bought the parts for the Cobra and that he hadn't turned a single page of the book.

But, without fail, he would always end the conversation with "I'll be revving up that engine soon, it's happening!" and "A book a week, that's how I stay so sharp!"

Ted genuinely *wanted* to learn, he wanted to grow . . . he just didn't *really* want to put in the actual work. Ted was the type of person who always says they will do something, from eating better to going to the gym more, but never follows through. Literally never.

Sound familiar? Sure it does. That's no knock on you or your loved ones who come to mind; that's actually *pretty normal*. It far from means you are a slouch. Life is busy—trust me, I get it. Unless you are living on a yacht cruising the South Pacific, the majority of us have a never-ending *to-do* list—something is bound to get bumped. It's just the way life is, right?

Ted, in fact, gets a lot done. He's always knocking another thing off "the list" and he's got the receipts to prove it. He's a total *to-do* checklist guy—and boy, does he LOVE to check off tasks. He loves it so much that he uses multiple apps that litter his phone with virtual checkmarks.

It's an amazing feeling, a real endorphin rush, to accomplish everything on your *to-do* list. I know, I'm a victim of it too. My personal weapon of choice? The sticky super-invention, *Post-Its*. Whether you make that final checkmark on your virtual list or crumple up the last sticky-note, finishing the daily to-dos makes you feel like a champion. Gives you that "sense of accomplishment" high.

Until you realize there's another list waiting for you around the corner tomorrow. An even more daunting list. Actually, if you don't get a jumpstart on it early (maybe even tonight!), you'll be treading water, barely keeping your head above the surface. It's not like you can just let things slide—if you do, then before you know it, things from last week's to-do list will have piled onto tomorrow's. Today's, tomorrow's, and yesterday's to-dos all blend into one giant pile of overwhelm stacked as high as the Empire State Building. Why does that *to-do* list never take a break? How are there so many things that need to constantly get done? It never stops!

I've been there! You've been there. Ted *lives there.*

And that morning, when he gave me his normal canned response about how it was all going to happen . . . next week, I just kind of snapped. Maybe it was the extra shot of espresso in my coffee or maybe I was just sick of seeing my friend act as if he was going to do things I knew he never would—a major pet peeve of mine.

"Ted, when are you actually going to do the things you say you want to do?"

Caught slightly off-guard, Ted choked a little on his vanilla latte before responding, "I'm going to do them, I just have to find the time. I have a to-do list the size of Alaska."

I knew that was my normative cue to agree with him, pat him on the back, and encourage him to continue plugging away at his *always growing, never-ending to-do list.* But I didn't.

"Ted," I said firmly, "make it happen. Put 'start the car building project with my son' and 'read a book' at the top of your to-do list. Actually, scrap your *to-do* list. You never get past your to-do list to any of the things you say you are going to accomplish. Forget the to-do list, you need a *to-grow* list."

The words just seemed to flow out of me while my throat burned from another gulp of piping hot coffee. But I didn't stop there.

Ted froze in shock as I snatched his phone, opened his app, and changed the title of his list from "Weekly To-Do's" to "Now To-Grow's." I was in the zone, the *put your foot down* intervention zone.

"Okay, fine, fine. I'll do it this week. I just have to get through Monday, and then I'll be able to start it on Tuesday . . ."

"No!" I nearly-yelled, lunging across the table and grabbing him firmly by both shoulders. "You. Start. Now. We're going to purchase the parts you need for the car, *right now*. And then we're going to get that book and we're reading the first chapter, out loud, together."

And that is exactly what we did.

The next day, I sent him a text: "To-grow vs. to-do, what are you choosing today, my man?"

He responded with emojis of a car and a book.

I sent him the same text the next day and the next day and the next, and, much like our coffee conversation, I always got the same response from him. Only, instead of an excuse and a promise to get to it eventually, now his recurring response was "I am doing it" with a selfie picture of his son and him working on the car together and the page he was currently on in his book.

Since that morning coffee eruption, Ted finished restoring the 1964 Shelby Cobra with his son and has even taken two weekend father-son road trips together in it. He's read thirty-one books and actually finished the book that had been the running joke itself, Victor Frankel's *Man's Search for Meaning*.

That's great and all, but it's not the car restoration or the number of books he's read that impresses me. I'm excited because Ted finally made the *mindset pivot* to control his list, rather than letting his list control him. He keeps a list now of things that help him *to-grow*, rather than having his time dictated by a list of things *to-do*. His goal isn't to keep his head barely above water, but to improve himself, to get excited about his life, to pursue his passions.

Now, don't get me wrong. I'm not condoning completely putting off your to-do list when there are things that absolutely need to be done throughout the day. You need to drop your kids off at school, you need to pick up groceries for the family, you need to do the laundry, you need to call about your health insurance to make sure it's renewed for the year. Yeah, you *have* to do these things! These are what I call to-do list *essentials*. The issue is that so many of us get caught up in the to-do list *non-essentials*. We fill our lists with *busywork*. The extra hour at the office on Saturday you *think* needs to be put in, the forty-five emails you *think* you need to send out before you can enjoy time with your family, and so many more things that we know aren't necessarily essential, but just "fillers" that keep us from what really means the most.

We have all been held captive by our *to-do* lists and that magical endorphin rush of checkmarks; we have all felt the stress and the anxiety of the list that never stops growing, no matter how many checkmarks we make.

Trust me, you will NEVER get everything done that you want to get done. *Boom.* Does that sound negative to you? Honestly, it's the most positive, freeing thought you can have. *You won't get everything done, and you don't have to.* Unchain yourself from the checkmarks; you can move, you can breathe. You are no longer a slave to what you *think* you have to get done; you are now free to what you *can* do. There will always be more on the list. Understanding that and being at peace with it gives you total control over *your* time.

One of the best lines I have ever heard is from my good friend and one of the top brain coaches in the world, Jim Kwik. He says, "The most important thing is to keep the most important thing the most important thing." That has stuck with me.

Every time you're getting ready to start another *to-do* list, just write *to-grow* at the top of the page. See how that simple word switch changes your priorities? That's your new *main* list. Not the old to-do, like everyone else in the world is bound to, but the new to-grow, where you can fully become the person you have always wanted to be.

You can fill it in with anything you'd like, as long as it will help you grow. Of course, get the *essentials* done, but don't you dare put a *non-essential busywork task* on there! Pay attention to how you feel when you put a checkmark by that list at the end of the day. Are you still exhausted and overwhelmed, or are you filled with a sense of joy, a sense of accomplishment that you just grew today in your passion, in something that you normally tell people you would love to have the time to do but are just *too busy*?

We don't have to be controlled by checkmarks; we can find joy, passion, and excitement in our *to-grow* lists. As uncommon as it might seem to mainstream society, we can prioritize the things we want to improve upon and learn about. We can choose to pivot our mindsets from *surviving with a to-do list* to *thriving with a to-grow list.*

FAILURE

BLUEPRINT ACTION PLAN

1. Create your own to-grow list! Next to the thermometer, write down three things you want to grow in this week. They can be anything, from learning a few new words in Spanish that you can use at your favorite tapas restaurant to working with your kids on some fifth-grade algebra that just looks like another language to you. (At this second, I'd probably choose reading one book of choice, learning one song to play on the guitar, and cooking a new meal I have never cooked before.) When you complete each one, fill in the space—by the end of the week, you'll be growing off the charts!

2. Write down "TO-GROW LIST" on a notecard and place it on your fridge or wherever you usually keep your to-do list alongside your current to-grow list itself. Commit to double-checking that you're checking off your to-grows for the day and/or week whenever you pass it.

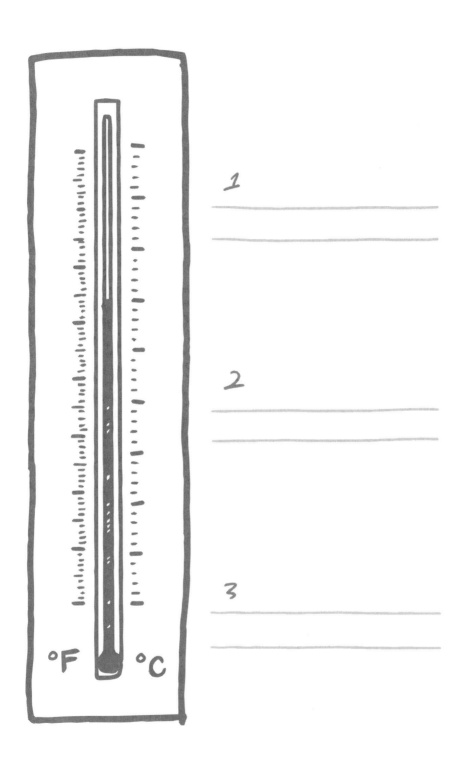

1 _____
  _____

2 _____
  _____

3 _____
  _____

DAY 22
SODOM'S APPLE

FIVE HOURS INTO HIKING THE mountains of Israel overlooking the Dead Sea, I was beyond taxed: hungry, thirsty, mentally drained. I had faithfully followed my tour guide up and down one dry barren mountain after another, and we'd finally arrived at a patch of green lushness. It looked like a rainforest on the surface of Mars. Praise the LORD!

Hanging from the tree right there in front of me was the juiciest piece of fruit I'd ever seen. I couldn't even identify what it was, but there was not a single doubt in my mind that it would taste *incredible*. Seriously, it was that beautiful and enticing, and I was DEFINITELY that hungry and thirsty.

I sprinted ahead of the small group to grab it, but my leader stopped me with an abrupt scream: "Don't eat that! It's poisonous!"

What? How could that gorgeous specimen be deadly?

My leader smiled at me and laughed. "Appearance on the outside isn't always what's at the core."

Of course he talked in parables. He was probably just mad I spotted it before him. Dibs.

He pulled out his Bible and began to read:

Thus says the Lord:
"Cursed is the man who trusts in man
and makes flesh his strength,
whose heart turns away from the Lord.
He is like a shrub in the desert,
and shall not see any good come.
He shall dwell in the parched places of the wilderness,
in an uninhabited salt land."

Translation? I'd just run up on the fruit of the Auricula Tree—aka Sodom's Apple.

"Ok, fine," I murmured, disappointment oozing out of my pores.

On we marched. Don't quote me on this, but I'm relatively positive we kept going for, give or take, about forty years.

At this point, I would have drank pure salt water from the Dead Sea. I dreamt of jumping in a pool of fresh water and drinking every last ounce of it, relaxing on the beach back home in Marina del Rey with a nice cold bottle of Gerolsteiner.

Finally, we came across a shrub that looked like it hadn't produced fruit for a few decades. On the leader's command, the group stopped and gathered around it as he opened his Bible again.

"Does this tree even have fruit?" I asked, very doubtfully.

Without answering, he read:

Blessed is the man who trusts in the Lord,
whose trust is the Lord.
He is like a tree planted by water,

SUCCESS

that sends out its roots by the stream,

and does not fear when heat comes,

for its leaves remain green,

and is not anxious in the year of drought,

for it does not cease to bear fruit.

He motioned for me to go ahead and take a branch.

Feeling almost bad for the bush, but also over the moon to quench my Sahara Desert thirst, I ripped a branch off and cracked it open, putting it directly into my mouth. I was expecting to get a few drops of water; instead, I got a steady stream of the best-tasting liquid to ever touch my lips. It filled and recharged me.

Despite hearing it approximately a billion times, I needed the trees of the mountains of Israel to slap me in the face with the message before I truly understood: no matter what things look like from the outside, it's what's on the inside that holds all the value.

I live my life with a ton of joy. Genuine joy, genuine excitement. I like to see the good and positive in things. But that's not how I've always been.

In 2010, I was in my last month of grad school at Western Illinois University, getting an MBA that was fully funded by my college basketball scholarship. I had been drafted to my uncle's NBA development team, and now I was going overseas to play professional basketball; everything was going my way. I had a great friend group; I was basically the big man on campus. On the surface, I literally had everything going for me.

So, why was I sitting in my parked car outside my apartment

complex at 10:32 PM, sobbing uncontrollably? Even I didn't even know at that moment, but it took me thirty-nine minutes to stop. I remember seeing that 11:11 on the clock vividly as I dried my last tears.

I was a good person. I worked hard. Sure, I partied and chased girls and occasionally drank a little too much, but I *was* in college—that's what college kids do, you know? But still, I woke up every morning feeling like a monster truck had run me over, then thrown it back in reverse for good measure. The physical side of the hangover hurt, but the emotional part dug even deeper.

I was broken. I had no joy. I had moments of happiness, yes, but they were fleeting. I thought I could find more, and I attempted to: a cruise to the Caribbean with the girl I was chasing, more partying, hanging around people who told me how good I was and encouraged my bad habits. But the things that seemed like they should be plugging up this gaping hole weren't satisfying anything. I was at rock bottom. I accepted any invitation to do literally anything just to get away from my lonely self.

One night, a freshman on the team, Billy, asked me to go to Fuel, some college hangout. Fine, whatever. It's not like I had anything to lose, and maybe I'd find the ticket to my happiness at this party, or at least something new to distract me.

We walked into a room filled with loud, joyful, passionate music—but not exactly club hits. I listened to the words for about twenty seconds and then looked over at Billy. This dude had brought me to a church group!

Fuel was a community of fellowship for people that followed

Christ—no particular religion, just people filled with the everlasting love of Jesus. Seemed pretty hokey to me. I didn't have a problem with the guy, but believing in God was something I'd planned on looking into when I was older and done having my "fun."

These people were clearly on drugs. Seriously, *a lot* of drugs. They were smiling, bouncing up and down, dancing, singing at the top of their lungs, praising this Jesus guy. (*Why does he get the praise? I want the praise.*) I was uncomfortable. I didn't want to sing, I didn't want to dance. I wanted to look each person in the eye and tell them to stop doing drugs! But I resisted out of sheer respect for Billy. I stood there for the entire ninety minutes, frozen, watching everyone around me.

When the speaker got up on stage to talk, everyone was silent and engaged. And when the time was up and the speaker had finished, everyone walked around, hugging each other, asking how the week was going and if there was anything in particular they could do to help and support one another.

Who goes out of their way to ask if they can support someone? That went completely against my conception of how you find happiness. Wasn't the point to get enough people to serve me until I was consistently comfortable? In my mind, comfort plus popularity equaled happiness.

I was extremely intrigued.

I came back the next week. And the next. And the next. I had to figure this out, this high. I had dabbled with marijuana in high school and college, but I'd never done any hard drugs. That was going to change, though. Whatever drug these people were on, I could tell it was the key to consistent, genuine joy. And I wanted it. Bad.

The fifth or sixth time I attended Fuel, a guy came over to Billy and me after the nightly activities had wrapped up, threw his arm around me, and asked me how my week had been.

"Pretty good," I shrugged, nonchalantly trying to cut the convo short and get away.

Just then, he wrapped me in a hug—a HUGE bear hug, cutting off any memory of oxygen. "I love you, brother."

I wanted out of that hug before it even started, but for some reason, the longer it lasted, the more I wanted to stay in that moment. I felt comforted, I felt as if the hole inside me had been filled. And not by the guy hugging me; someone far, far greater had His arms around me. Whether or not I wanted to admit it at that time, I knew it was Jesus. He had me.

Now, I'm not telling you this story to try to force you to think you have to believe in Jesus as your savior. If that's meant to be, then it will happen for you through Him.

Here's the thing—we all produce fruit. In some way, shape, or form, we find and give nourishment to those around us. But not every fruit is a *good* fruit. The fruit that we produce and consume can be absolutely poisonous. And if we truly stop and think about it, most of us produce poisonous fruit at some point throughout our days.

When others gossip, do we feed fuel to the fire and gossip right along? When we know others are making bad decisions, do we step up and confront them, or do we let them ingest that poison because it's *not our business*? When no one is watching, do we make our

SUCCESS

poisonous fruit as attractive as that Sodom's apple, enticing others around us so that we can use them for our personal gain?

Is that the type of fruit you produce? Is that the type of fruit you *want* to produce? Only you can answer that question for yourself; only you truly know, deep down, who you are and who you are striving to be.

Even though I thought I was a good person, I produced poisonous fruit and gorged myself on other people's poisonous fruit; despite that, I was starving to death. I lived very selfishly, only caring about what I could get from others and how I could secure fleeting happiness from life's tempestuous highs. Nothing was genuine for me; nothing was real. I found myself constantly lying to myself, which led to lying to others, my friends, my family. I was living a life that could be viewed as great on the outside, but on the inside, it was a life of extreme quiet desperation; I was dying.

When I saw the fruit that Billy and the people at Fuel were producing, I was so poisoned and malnourished, I mistook their joy for drugs. They were generous and supportive and loving; they had a bounty to share. By following their example, by following Christ's example, I learned how to produce the same type of healthy, joyous, positive fruit. Sure, it wasn't always as attractive on the outside, but it felt so, so much better on the inside. Let me tell you, nothing, *absolutely* nothing, is better.

We all have this challenge in our life: we all want to look as if we are doing "good" in the eyes of society, in the eyes of our peers. We wonder if we're doing better than the person next to us, if we are "better" than our neighbor. We think, *I'll surely reap the benefits if I look like I'm doing good.* But what is really inside of us? Are we concerned with doing good for a bigger purpose? Out of genuine love and care for others? Do we have a servant mentality and pour ourselves into others without expecting anything in return? When we start producing joyous fruit, we stop caring or worrying about what others think of us, what society thinks of us, or what our peers think of us. We know that we have something pure, genuine, and everlasting that we want to share with those around us.

There are many types of fruit; some lead us down the path of destruction and some lead us to joy, fulfillment, and peace. The question isn't *if* you are going to produce fruit, the question is *what* type of fruit are you going to make?

BLUEPRINT ACTION PLAN

1. It can be tough in the moment to tell when you're producing rotten fruit—it can feel very much like business as usual! We're all human, and we all do it—but there's ways to quit, and even more ways to turn your rotten fruit into something life-giving and nourishing for you and everyone you encounter.

In the pieces of fruit, write down three specific examples of when you've put negative things into the world. You might not be able to take them back, but you know you can avoid doing them again in the future! Now, follow the arrows and brainstorm how you can turn even your rotten fruit into something better, and write your idea down in the pie. Although this type of self-examination is grueling, it's crucial to doing better, being better, and feeling much, much better!

2. Write down "WHAT TYPE OF FRUIT AM I PRODUCING?" on a notecard and put it near the bowl, pantry, or fridge drawer where you keep your fruit at home. Each time you reach for a piece of fruit (which should definitely happen at least once a day!), commit to reflecting on the positive and negative things you have put into the world today.

227

DAY 23
TURTLE LIFE

I'M A SELF-ADMITTED TYPE A personality: a go-getter to the max. I want things to happen IMMEDIATELY! Not tomorrow, not in a week, but now. Let's just say patience isn't my strongest virtue. We all know the story of the tortoise and the hare, slow and steady wins the race, but honestly, I always got frustrated by that as a kid. Why couldn't the hare just go all out without stopping and resting? He would have surely won the race then, right?

What I didn't realize, when I was in fourth grade bemoaning another agonizing defeat for the hare, is that the story is an analogy for life: *play the long game or you will flame out quickly.*

Easy to read, tough to implement.

At fifty-one, Nick Nurse, my uncle, role model and mentor, became the head coach of the 2018-2019 NBA Champion Toronto Raptors. A first year head coach winning the NBA Championship is about as common as a unicorn. Everyone saw how fast the assistant coach rose to the top and thought, "Oh wow, overnight success!" If they only knew even a quarter of the story . . .

Nick was handed the coaching reins at tiny Grandview University in Des Moines, Iowa, when he was twenty-three, but he'd already set out to become an NBA head coach years before— that was his mission and he was determined. From Des Moines, his journey took him to South Dakota University as a college assistant before he went international. He became the head player/coach of the Birmingham Bullets in England (a country that could literally care less about basketball) followed by the Manchester Giants, followed by the London Towers. He came back to the States to coach the Oklahoma Storm in a league that doesn't even exist anymore, and then once again headed back across the pond to England to run the Brighton Bears. Finally, he returned to North America for good with the newly formed and "hope it works out" NBA D-League expansion team the Iowa Energy. The next stop was down south to the border of Mexico, to coach for the Rio Grande Valley Vipers. He journeyed beyond basketball obscurity, to say the least.

Then, he FINALLY landed in the NBA, nearly twenty-five years after he set out on the journey, as an assistant with the Toronto Raptors.

To claim that all happened overnight? Not a chance. Nick's journey is almost the perfect example of one of my favorite quotes: "It takes ten years to become an overnight success." Just, in Nick's case, it was twenty-five.

I was too young to fully remember the England days of Nick's journey, but I do vividly remember the NBA D-League days in Iowa and Texas. I watched a person who was so good at his craft and so smart be overlooked and underappreciated. I can't even count the mornings that Nick would tell me that he had a potential opportunity coming up with an NBA team over our mugs of freshly brewed Folgers coffee (I credit Nick with creating my coffee addiction), only to see it unfold in the exact opposite way he'd hoped.

I remember stories Nick would tell in the evenings while we were cooking less-than-gourmet dinners together (at least we tried!) about coaching overseas in a desolate gym for a team with no fans. He basically had to play the role of trainer (taping ankles), team manager (lining up the games and picking up the players from their homes), team GM (making the deals to sign players), and of course, coach (wrangling players who didn't even play basketball as their real job). Shoot, he'd even make the popcorn for the concession stands half the time.

One morning, Nick said something to me that I will never forget: "David, if I were to do this whole journey over again, I wouldn't change a darn thing. I know I'll be ready when my time comes; I've prepared my whole life for it. It's just a matter of time. It's coming. Remember this, David: never take the elevator, always take the stairs. Nothing that means something comes quickly. It's all step by step. Every day, it's one more step up the stairs."

Nick played the long game. Nick was the tortoise. As much as I'm sure he sometimes wanted to be the hare, he did something every single day that would bring him one step closer to fulfilling his dream. He never gave up, even though there were so many times that anyone in their "right mind" would think about a career change. But Nick didn't care; he persevered. He knew what his goal was, and nothing was going to stop him from reaching it. Even if it took twenty-five years and millions of miles.

Nick did it; he got to the top. He achieved his goal and is currently thriving as one of the best coaches in the NBA. And not one bit of it was luck. Step by step, he *prepared for opportunity.*

I guess that's probably why I always prefer to take the stairs.

Even if I'm trying to get to the twelfth floor of a building. It might be a little extreme, but it constantly reminds me that everything is a process, everything is a journey, and nothing worth anything is going to happen overnight. The elevator to the top relies on so many things that could go wrong: electricity, technology, man-made errors that could strand you for hours or even send you crashing back down to the ground. But not stairs; stairs give you the control, the power, and the satisfaction. When you make it to the top, you feel the burn in your legs. That's accomplishment.

Everything is a long game. No matter how much I want it and no matter how hard I try to make it happen right away, it doesn't. And it won't. It's just not on my timing—it's all on God's timing. The best timing.

If you achieve your goals very quickly right away, that means one of two things:

1. You didn't set your goals high enough and you should reevaluate, or

2. You probably aren't as prepared for the situation as you should be and it will flame out faster than you would like.

The tortoise knew his game plan: step by step, slow and steady wins the race. Nick knew his game plan, and step by step, he did the best he could every single day with the situation he was given. Whether he was in Brighton, England, in a city that barely knew what a basketball was, or on the border of Mexico, where the only reason people came to the game was to get free tacos if the team scored 100, he just kept making himself better. Nick has seen it all, been through it all, and rose to the top of his profession. Not by sheer luck, not by the stars aligning, but by playing the long game. Step by step.

BLUEPRINT ACTION PLAN

1. On the elevator floor indicator, fill out the penthouse with something incredible you were given in life well before you were prepared for it—something you were so excited to get, but that fizzled out quickly.

   On each of the floors, write down something that, in hindsight, you would develop (or have since developed) that would have been beneficial to bring to that opportunity—something you wish you'd had the chance to prepare.

   What opportunity are you preparing for now?

2. Write down "TAKE THE STAIRS, NOT THE ELEVATOR" on a notecard and place it close the staircase in your house you use the most. Commit to reflecting on your daily steps and long-term plays each time you hit the stairs.

DAY 24
SCRUBBING FECES & RUNNING BAREFOOT

IT WAS LATE FEBRUARY 2015, and the wind off the harbor pierced my skin as I tossed my car keys to the attendant working at the Newark Airport VIP. Two bellhops grabbed my bags to load onto the chartered Brooklyn Nets plane. A warm winter jacket was thrown around my shoulders, and I was almost coddled by attendants for the thirty-foot walk directly to the plane. I took the stairs all by myself, though.

The private jet was the pinnacle of luxury. I strolled down the aisle, then draped my stuff strategically to claim an entire row to stretch out and relax. I went to the back of the plane to fill a plate with roasted sea bass, smoked salmon, and a plethora of grilled-to-perfection vegetables. As I slid into my seat, I popped open the top-of-the-line laptop the Nets provided for me to watch game film of the upcoming opponent . . .

But the flight's Wi-Fi *wasn't high speed.*

Sure, it was working, but at 1990's speed. Seriously? Ridiculous.

I called over the young, scared flight attendant and let him have it. He nodded as he took the verbal abuse, and when I was done, without saying a word, he walked back to the front of the plane.

Fuming, I caught a glimpse of fellow Nets employees, wide-eyed, mouthing the word "whoa" to themselves.

And that's when it hit me, like an anvil dropping on my head from a mile high: I was extremely entitled.

Someone else had parked my car and swaddled me in a warm winter jacket that wasn't even mine; I was fully extended across multiple seats of a private plane, stuffing my face with gourmet foods, *berating a young flight attendant because the Wi-Fi wasn't the highest speed possible.*

What happened to me?!? Where was the humble cornfed Iowa boy who was thankful for everything and never took anything for granted?

I'd been in the job for just over a month, but it had been a month of chartered flights, five-star hotels, and lobster and filet mignon dinners. I was spoiled. Extremely spoiled, and it happened extremely fast.

It ate at me throughout the rest of the season; I knew it was there, lingering like a shadow in the dark. At times, I would even remind others how grateful we should be for all of this. But it was just hot air coming out of my mouth. I wasn't living it. I was pretending to be someone better, signaling my virtue without feeling it. I knew I needed a wake-up call, but I was fully immersed in every human comfort you could imagine and I didn't want to give any of it up.

My wake-up call came like a shovel to the forehead, which I am so thankful for now. Being released from my coaching position at the end of the season was probably one of the best things that ever happened to me. No more private chartered flights, no more five-star hotels, no more filet mignons. All of that was over. And somehow, I found myself on a plane to Africa, Kenya and Uganda, the heart of some of the poorest slums on earth.

Packed into a middle seat like a sardine, I arrived in Kampala, Uganda, thirteen hours after take-off. The hot equator sun beat down on my neck as I walked off the plane into what felt like a microwave oven crusted with year-old-fish smell.

I trudged on through the next ten days in Kampala and Nairobi, witnessing kids wear the same hand-me-down clothes that I had given them day after day because they didn't have any other options. I watched shoeless children run up and down a basketball court that looked like an earthquake had just hit it with huge smiles on their faces. I watched mothers balance fruit baskets and water on their heads and hold their little ones' hands as they walked miles through town. I watched a community sharing and giving, without a single hand taking or stealing. I sat in circles of villagers slurping down goat broth soup and piling in rice and mitoki (a native form of mushed up plantains). I laughed, I cried, I held and hugged the little bodies of sick, malnourished children. I picked up stone after stone to build a shelter near the basketball court where kids could stay if they had no family left. I walked through slums; I danced in the streets; I slept in huts.

What I found was life-changing and exactly what I needed. These were the most joyful people I had ever been around. Ever. And they had nothing I had previously thought was so vital to life. There wasn't anyone to carry my bags, no gourmet buffets, no pillow-top comfy bed—there wasn't even a pillow. But there was love, gratitude, a sense of community, and a feeling of absolute servanthood. The people of Kenya and Uganda opened my eyes to what life is really about: genuinely pouring yourself into others. *Pour into others and you will be filled.*

At another point in my travels, I didn't think I had much left of myself to pour into anyone (unless some buckets of sweat would have helped). I was in pain. I'd just thrown out my lower back at a basketball clinic the day before; bending down to tie my shoes was a ten-minute agony-infused chore. It was almost midnight, and I was drenched from the moment I stepped off the plane. It smelled like being knee deep in a dumpster, only worse. A torrent of beeping car horns rained from the night sky. Calcutta, India, inundated and overwhelmed me in five minutes flat.

Calcutta, home of Mother Teresa, is one of the poorest places on the face of the planet. My younger brother had been living there as a missionary for the past year, and he'd asked me to come visit him and experience the culture. I just so happened to be in the area—well, in Southeast Asia at least, running basketball coaching clinics throughout the Philippines, Hong Kong, and Singapore. I scheduled four days in India before I flew to Japan to continue my jet-setting quest to teach basically everyone in every Asian country how to shoot a basketball.

After a less-than-rejuvenating four hours' sleep in a puddle of my own sweat on a literal block of wood and something that halfway resembled a pillow, I was up at 5 AM, ready to go.

"Should I shower?" I yelled downstairs at my brother.

"No need, trust me," he responded with a slight chuckle.

The mission group met up, and we were on our way. I asked

multiple people where we were going, but the only response I got was "Kalighat." That didn't mean anything to me, of course.

We grabbed chai by the side of the road, dodged traffic like we were in the old videogame Frogger (seriously, crossing the road in India is a game of life and death), and packed ten people into a rickshaw that was probably fit for four.

As we drove or scooted or Fred Flintstone-ran (whatever you want to call it) along in the rickshaw, the people on the streets nearly brought me to tears. They were living in ditches, scrounging around for food, literally dying right in front of my eyes. I'd seen poverty, but nothing like this. The sunken eyes of desperation pierced me as we drove through the city; the smells were worse than the night before. Have you ever smelled someone actively dying of neglect? I did that day, many times.

When we got there, I was given gloves and an apron and ordered to get into the kitchen.

This should be easy, I thought. *I'll probably just be serving food to the homeless; I've done this before.*

The first person who was brought to me had one leg, was covered in his own feces, and was dry heaving constantly.

"What do I do?" I screamed.

My brother was nowhere in sight; he was busy at work. He'd been here many times before and was one of the leaders. I guess he just assumed I would figure it out on my own. Mark that down as part of the learning experience.

This one-legged man was visibly near death. I took him into the back of the "kitchen" and turned on the hose, power-washing him from head to toe. At least he was clean now. Sort of. I stared at him, and he stared at me.

What now? I wondered.

What now was something I wasn't expecting: the dry heaves turned into a not-so-dry-heave of everything inside of him, plus a mucus/blood combo that still makes my stomach quiver. I stood there, covered in it, in shock and complete disbelief.

After my brain kicked into gear again, I turned on the hose and washed myself all over, twice. No, maybe five times. It was only 7:30 in the morning.

At that moment, I figured out where I was: a death and reviving house. This was where they brought people they'd rescued off the street who were barely alive and tried to save them. Some don't make it, but many do. And if they do, it's all thanks to the people who put others far before themselves, people who understand the servant attitude of *character over comfort.* There aren't any newspaper articles written about these people, no monetary bonuses, no awards or even pats on the back from a superior. It's a mission, it's a lifestyle, it's the epitome of losing one's self to help others.

Think about the most joyful times in your life. Do any of them involve earning a lot of money? Can you remember that time you got a big fat paycheck and cashed it in and were super content for months and months after? Probably not.

Do these most joyful memories involve giving to others and feeling a sense of purpose? Some of the greatest human beings to ever walk the earth were *servants:* Jesus, Nelson Mandela, Martin Luther King Jr., Mother Teresa. They gave so much, losing their identities

239

in the genuine care for others; in turn, they found out exactly who they were and the greater purpose that they were made for.

But it doesn't come easy. To develop this *servant* attitude, you have to accept that first, there will be character growth. Character over comfort.

Choosing *character over comfort* is the only way to grow. Not everyone has to dive into full-on mission trips to India and Africa, but if we stay in our little worlds that revolve around us, then we stay small. We go through the motions, never growing, never fully understanding what it is to give. When you immerse yourself in something that throws you out of your comfort zone, you grow. I grew that day in Calcutta, India, more than I had in the prior twenty-five years of my life.

If there is one thing in life that can steal your joy, it's entitlement. We all have felt it; some of us, unfortunately, make it an absolute staple of our lives. Entitlement is why people with enormous bank accounts and famous names, who we think should be the most content and happy, often go through life in absolute misery. *Entitlement is the thief in the night that robs tomorrow's daily joy.* That statement has so much impact on me; it shapes who I am. I have it written on the dry-erase board that hangs above my coffee pot so I can see it every morning when I wake up. I let it sink in and impact how I live out my day—WITHOUT the chains of entitlement around my ankles.

I learned the hard way. I had to pivot to treating each day as an absolute gift from God that I am beyond blessed to have, realizing I am entitled to nothing and should be grateful for everything.

Sure, from time to time, I'll catch myself wondering why I don't have this or why I don't have that. But then I'm able to picture so many people—like the man in the Kalighat, or the little boy who was dying of starvation in Uganda yet still wore a huge smile, kissed me on the cheek, and whispered "I love you" directly into my ear—and I remember my true place in this world.

If we think that we're owed something, we wear this attitude on our sleeves. But if we are thankful and grateful, our daily joy will increase beyond our wildest imaginations. Trust me, I am living proof.

BLUEPRINT ACTION PLAN

1. Gratitude is one of the best antidotes to entitlement, and the quickest way to build your gratitude muscle is to examine where you've let it go lax.

Think about your day yesterday; in the stick figure, write down one person you took for granted. What did they do for you, and why did you brush that off? How might your day have changed for the worse if they hadn't been in it? How do you wish you had shown your gratitude? When I think about it, I realize I need to do a better job showing my gratitude for the young interns who rebound when I work out the NBA players. I get to coach and pass while they chase down every shot. Without them, the workouts wouldn't be even close to as effective as they are!

Now, think about the past week; inside the key, write an opportunity you took for granted—maybe even complained about! Believe it or not, at times I complain about working with too many players, completely forgetting what an incredible opportunity this is. In reality, the agents make my life easy. I never have to find a gym to use, the weight room and high-level recovery are provided, and everything is set up better than I could imagine on my own.

Finally, pinpoint a lifetime gift that you haven't expressed proper gratitude for and write it down in the present. For example, I am super blessed to have Taylor as my wife, and I don't take her for granted for a second—but she didn't get here by herself! Her parents raised her to become the woman I love. I wouldn't have my wife without her parents!

For each of these examples, come up with one way you can express your gratitude today—get out of your comfort zone and build your character with some genuine thanks!

2. Write down "ENTITLEMENT IS THE THIEF IN THE NIGHT THAT ROBS TOMORROW'S DAILY JOY" on a notecard and place it on your bed stand next to the last light you turn off each day. Commit to reflecting on the nature of entitlement and banishing it from your life each time you touch that lamp.

DAY 25

A 98 MPH FASTBALL & A FIFTH OF VODKA

I WAS SURPRISED WHEN TED asked if we could grab dinner. Not only was it a deviation from our usual weekend morning coffee, it was already late and I knew he was supposed to leave for Disney World the next morning. He and his family had been planning the trip for months; to be honest, I think he'd been looking forward to it nearly as much as the kids. His daughter was eleven and his son was nine, both pretty prime Disney ages, so that's really saying something!

The moment I walked into the restaurant and saw Ted's face, I knew something was very wrong.

"Hey buddy, what's going on?"

"Report cards came out," Ted said, burying his head in his hands.

Now, Ted never talked much about his childhood, but I knew he hadn't been the most studious kid. He'd gotten middle-of-the-pack, average grades. Later in life, he'd regretted that; he'd dreamt of becoming an engineer, and he felt like his options had been limited because he'd never paid enough attention to school. He wanted the absolute best for his own kids, and he was determined that his son and daughter didn't sell themselves short.

This wasn't the first time there had been some report card drama. Ted's kids tried hard in school, but their passion to get straight A's wasn't as high as their passion for reading books they actually enjoyed or playing on their soccer teams. After all, they *were* kids. That was never something Ted wanted to hear, though, so I was surprised he was bringing this to me.

The grade review process was always the same, and it sounded completely awful: when report cards came home in the mail, the kids were responsible for opening them at the table and reading their grades out loud before dinner started. Every grade below an A meant twenty spankings. (Yeah, probably not the best parenting move on Ted's part.)

On this evening, his son had opened his report card first: two A's and 3 B's, the worst grades he'd brought home all year. Tears welled up in his eyes as he realized there were sixty intense spankings coming his way, but he did everything in his power to choke them back.

Ted's daughter, who'd been a straight A student the entire year, opened her report card very slowly, then quickly put it back in the envelope, refusing to read it out loud as she began to cry. She had no A's—five B's.

"I beat them, David," Ted said, fighting to hold back tears of his own. "I struck them. I struck them harder than I ever have. My daughter, I spanked her 100 times. I'd never spanked her before."

He started to sob violently. I got up and walked around to his side of the table and rested my hand on his shoulder. I didn't say a word; I just stood there and listened.

"My wife tried to pull me back, she tried to tell me to take it easy on them, but I couldn't. There was something in me that wouldn't stop. I hate myself for it, I'll never forgive myself."

Ted sat there for the next fifteen minutes with his head in his arms, crying. It was the most vulnerable I had ever seen him.

When he'd let every last tear out of his system and finally sat up, he looked at me. I knew he wanted me to tell him everything would be okay, but I couldn't.

"Why did you do it?"

He was in obvious pain and my question caught him off guard; in that moment, he was able to respond honestly. He told me a story he'd buried deep down long ago.

Ted was supposed to be a professional baseball player—at least, that's what his dad thought. Ted actually didn't even enjoy playing baseball. But every morning, Ted and his father would go outside in the front yard. Ted's father taught him the intricacies of a curveball, a slider, and even the rarely-thrown-in-any-league pitch, a screwball. There were simulated games with tighter-than-tight strike zones and speed guns tracking Ted's fastball, all holding him to a major league standard. And if Ted didn't strike out three imaginary players in a row, then the "game" of toss with his father would continue until Ted couldn't feel his arm. Finally, when Ted was allowed to return to the house, his father would say the words he dreaded most: "I'll meet you at the field after school." Two workouts a day, more intense than what a Triple-A minor leaguer battling to make it up to the majors would put himself through. And Ted was nine.

Against his desire, Ted played in high school. From the outside looking in, Ted was the man, an All-State baseball player with multiple college scholarship offers. Inside, Ted's hatred for base-ball continued to grow, as did his resentment and hatred for his father. But that didn't stop his father from basically bullying him into signing on the dotted line and locking his fate in for four more years of baseball at the college level. Ted literally prayed at night that no professional scouts would think he was good enough for the major leagues. He drank, like many college kids do, but a couple of beers a night evolved into an entire twelve pack and eventually into a fifth of vodka. It was the only escape he could find from baseball, from his father, and from his father's crushing expectations.

It all came spiraling down one horrific day in October during Ted's sophomore year. He was set to pitch against his team's conference rivals. The matchup was between the two rising star pitchers to duel it out in front of multiple MLB scouts.

Ted didn't show up. He couldn't. He was in a self-induced alcohol-poisoned coma.

One of the assistant coaches came looking for Ted, since he'd missed the morning team meeting and pre-game brunch. He found Ted passed out unconscious on his dorm room floor, and in an absolute panic, he called 911. Ted was rushed to the hospital.

The news came out: "Star pitcher hospitalized for alcohol poisoning." MLB scouts were no longer interested in Ted. Neither was his father. He didn't visit the hospital. He didn't even call to check how Ted was doing. Ted didn't see or hear from his father for over seven months, and their relationship has never been repaired. Ted never picked up a baseball again.

"David, I've become my father," Ted cried.

"No, you haven't. Ted, tonight, you can let yourself go from who he was and what he did to you. You can be free. What you just did there, telling me that entire story, that's your freedom." I paused, then continued, "You haven't ever told anyone what happened to you, have you?"

"No," he responded. "You're the first person."

I told Ted to go home and tell his wife, and most importantly, to tell his kids. "Be vulnerable. Let them know why you did what you did and why it isn't going to happen ever again. You can make things right. You can mend these relationships. But first you have to be vulnerable. *Victory goes to the vulnerable.*"

Ted took this advice. He went home that night and told his wife everything. They stayed up until 3 AM, crying together and holding each other. They woke up early the next morning and made the kids their favorite fluffy-butter-and-way-too-much-syrup pancakes, and Ted shared everything with them. He promised he would never spank them again. They booked new tickets to Disney World, and they went to the magic land to spend time as a family—a family that loved each other very much. One that could make mistakes and grow closer together from them, one that didn't allow differences to build up and create a lifetime of resentment, and one that forgave and did not punish vulnerability.

We all have things we have kept inside us for far too long— maybe, like Ted, even suppressed for our *entire* lives. Think about the most freeing times in your life. I'm guessing you weren't having a surface-level conversation. You laid your shield on the ground and opened yourself up, taking the chance of being judged, scorned, laughed at, pointed at, and looked down on; instead, you found freedom.

We all want to be vulnerable, even if we don't admit it. We want to be ourselves—who we are and who we were made to be. We want to free ourselves of the bondage of expectations, of not fitting in, of falling flat on our face and failing.

This is a mindset we pivot without making any major overhauls, but it makes all the difference in how we feel about ourselves and how we relate to the world. Take the shield down; it only protects you from the judgment of people who do not matter, and it keeps you from fully loving and being loved by the people who do. Just a small turn of the dial makes all the difference. Be vulnerable. *Victory goes to the vulnerable.*

BLUEPRINT ACTION PLAN

1. On the balloon, write down one thing that you have been holding inside. One thing that pains you to think about, something that you don't want to let anyone else see or know. Possibly something from your childhood you have kept built up within yourself for years.

Inside the scissors, write down how you are going to cut the string that ties you to your balloon, to let it out and let it go. The only way to free yourself of the past that burdens you is to be vulnerable. Trust me, you will feel a GREAT weight lifted off your shoulders. To be able to love yourself fully, you need to be able to be vulnerable.

2. Write down "VICTORY GOES TO THE VULNERABLE" on a notecard and tape it to the top of your trashcan lid as a reminder to throw away the hurtful things you are holding inside of you.

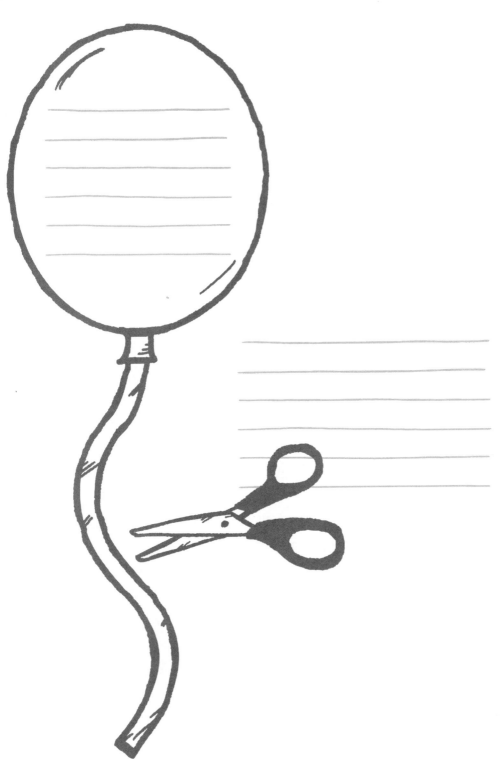

DAY 26

THE GREATEST ONES YOU'VE NEVER HEARD OF

THE BASKETBALL WORLD IS JUST like any other major industry—large, but also very small. Through the six-degrees-of-separation, I developed a close relationship with the Phil Jackson of Philippines basketball, legendary Tim Cone. Tim invited me to fly down to work with his team for a week and help develop his basketball players in Manila . . . but really, I think he just invited me down there out of the kindness of his heart. You see, I was only twenty-six; Tim had won nearly as many championships as the number of years I'd been alive. Tim is a mega icon in the Philippines—everywhere we went, he was mobbed by fans. But you would never know it by talking to him, as he is one of the most humble and caring people I have ever met.

Now, Manila's far from a small town, but somehow, the second something happens, everyone already knows about it. Word got out that Tim had brought in a young shooting coach to help his team, and if the best coach in basketball was doing it, then it just made sense for everyone else to want to do it too. Including Manny Pacquiao.

Tim is definitely a celebrity, but Manny is famous on an entirely different level. The boxing icon-turned-senator-turned-boxer-again-turned-senator-again is a huge basketball fan, just like everyone else in the Philippines. But unlike many others, Manny has the means to own a team, be the GM for the team, coach the team (kind of), and play for the team (less kind of). Word got around that I was working with Tim's team, and as his competitor, Manny wanted what the best had. So, he invited me to meet with him and work with his team for a day.

With Tim's stamp of approval and encouragement, I did. It was one of those experiences when you just have to pause, breathe, and pinch yourself to check if it's really happening.

The team driver picked me up from Tim's house and brought me to practice. When I arrived at the gym, Manny was there to meet me. He stuck out his hand rather timidly and quietly said in broken English, "Nice to meet you, help my team win."

One of the higher-pressure introductions I've ever had, especially from the man with the most lethal left hook on the planet. I told him I'd do my best, and I threw on my shoes and got to work on the court. There were a lot of players packed into the humid, muggy, 1960s gym, but I still ran them through every high energy and game action drill I knew.

When practice ended, Manny's manager (whom I had become fast friends with due to his ability to speak English) took me back to an office to sit down and talk with Manny.

It was nothing like I expected.

I anticipated a stand-offish, full-of-himself multi-millionaire boxing icon; what I saw was a genuine, caring, loving human being who wanted nothing more than for his people to have hope and love. All Manny talked about was how he could help his team. The questions he asked didn't pertain to himself or anything he could gain in the basketball world, but what he could do for his players,

SUCCESS

253

his coaches, and everyone in the organization. He wanted to make a difference in their lives.

He grew up in the slum-ridden Bukidnon province, one of the most dangerous areas in the Philippines; he boarded a ship to escape to Manila as a teenager, leaving his family to pursue the dream of becoming a professional boxer when all the odds were stacked against him. He earned world fame and stardom, securing the option to live a lavish life outside of his home country, but instead, he poured everything he had back into his people and his family. He became a savior to his countrymen, a beacon of hope and a ray of light. They didn't always have much, but they had Manny.

There's a big chance that Manny doesn't think about that day we met; I doubt he'd recognize me today if we passed on the street. But I'll carry the impact he had on me for the rest of my life.

Manny's accomplishments in boxing and politics will outlive him; they will be recorded in history books and passed down through future generations. He will leave a legacy, in the way we've all been conditioned to correlate the terms success and legacy. All of the "greats," from Martin Luther King Jr. to George Washington to Mother Teresa, have their deeds recorded, but based off what I've seen and come to understand about true legacies, those deeds fail to paint the true definition of what legacy actually is. The achievements that these icons produced are merely by-products of the main thing that made these people great . . . which is that they genuinely poured themselves into others.

We all want to leave a legacy. Whether we admit it out loud or not, deep down, we all want to be remembered for something great. We all have dreams of leaving a mark on the world like Abe Lincoln or C.S. Lewis. We fantasize that billboards touting our accomplishments will tower over cities worldwide, our stories will be repeated as legendary tales, movies will be made about us, and we will be endlessly celebrated. Nothing crazy, just a day on the calendar named in our honor, maybe a parade or two. There's still a little space on Mt. Rushmore, right?

Sorry, not going to happen.

The truth is, you almost certainly won't be remembered 100 years from now. No one will know you ever existed, much less any of the things you have accomplished. Think about it—do you know the name of your great-great-grandfather and grandmother? What were their proudest accomplishments? Do you know the name of the people who built your home with their bare hands? Who designed the roads you drive on every day? Who were the senators in your home state the year you were born? All of these people left visible legacies, but very few people are celebrated in timeless perpetuity.

Aiming to create a legacy that will make you famous is a losing proposition. It might work for a while, but that flame will burn out quickly, and the daily battle of watching your back for the next quick-riser who could dethrone you will eat at your soul. However, if you stop for a second and completely untie the relationship between legacy and fame and focus instead on positively impacting the ones around you, there's no telling how many lives you can touch.

Sometimes the most unassuming people leave the biggest and most lasting impact. And that's great news for all of us; we don't have to come from money, go to a prestigious college, be handed fame, or be given literally anything to have a life-changing effect on the people around us and potentially millions and millions of others.

Unless you are a basketball savant and know the ins and outs of every NBA coaching staff, you've probably never heard of Ron Adams. But the greatest team of all time, one of the greatest dynasties ever assembled in sports, would have never been if it wasn't for Ron. Some of the greatest coaches in the NBA, leaders like Steve Kerr, Tom Thibodeau, George Karl, and Brad Stevens, would not be who they are today if it wasn't for Ron. Some of the greatest players of a generation, household names such as Steph Curry, Kevin Durant, Russell Westbrook, and Derrick Rose, wouldn't be who they are without Ron.

Shouldn't he parading around, beating his chest over his accomplishments, constantly thanked and praised for being the backbone of so many success stories? Shouldn't there already be books written about him, documentaries made about him, and billboards with his face on them?

Trust me, that's the last thing Ron would want. He takes no credit for any of this.

Ron doesn't want you to know about him; in fact, he didn't even want me to write about him in this book. I had to twist his arm and then some for permission!

Ron has been a mentor to me, though I'm not fully sure why; I know I didn't do anything to deserve it. Ron is a truth teller, for better or for worse. At times, it's frustrated me, but then I always come back around to realize that yeah, Ron was right. Again.

Ron took me under his wing the first day I met him, at a high school gym on an oven-baked July day in Las Vegas. Golden State was going through their summer league practice, when the majority of NBA teams come together for ten days with their young players, rookies, and potential last roster spot vets battling for a contract. It's a place where young coaches are able to work on their craft and learn in actual game situations. (And also play way too much blackjack into the late hours of the 120-degree Vegas nights.)

Ron was an assistant coach with the up-and-coming Warriors (the year they first became THE dynasty Warriors). I was allowed to be in the gym during closed private practices as the shooting coach for then-rookie James McAdoo. I had no idea who Ron was, but we shared an obvious passion for shooting, and we quickly fell into a deep conversation about the intricacies of elbow placement and follow-through finish on a basketball player's jump shot.

I saw that Ron genuinely loved what he did and every player he worked with. James was an undrafted rookie, but Ron still treated him the way he would have treated an NBA All-Star. He was in Vegas at NBA Summer League because he *wanted* to be there, not because he *had* to be there. And while he certainly loved the game of basketball, it didn't define who he was.

Ron is a renaissance man with many interests, but all of them center on making the world a better place and helping others improve in their passions. I know that sounds cliché, but Ron legitimately wants to empower others. He's a quiet activist who stands up for what he believes in without caring what others think. Ron's as excited to talk about philosophy, religion, sociology, and politics as he is basketball. He understands the big picture; he

SUCCESS

understands that we aren't here for our own personal gain in whatever our chosen profession might be.

Years after the first time I met Ron, we were at his favorite local coffee shop in Oakland, within walking distance from the Warriors practice facility. As we sat there, sipping coffee and talking about the bean of the day, the conversation flowed into European travel, Michelin-rated restaurants we had been to, the current state of the economy, and the philanthropic foundations he's involved in. In that hour and a half conversation, the game of basketball did not come up. Not once did he talk about how he helped mastermind the greatest offensive and defensive combination ever in the NBA, or the back-to-back NBA championships he had just won, or how he'd just received the NBA Assistant Coach of the Year Award. No mention of how he mentored the top head coaches currently in the NBA or developed some of the best players. Basketball didn't remotely come up at all until we were about to get our bill and leave.

"How's James doing?" Ron asked.

"Great," I said. "Just had a baby girl, couldn't be happier."

Ron's grin eclipsed the massive diamond-encrusted championship ring on his finger.

And that's Ron Adams.

Ron has created a legacy that will live on forever. No, it's not what the world wants us to think a legacy is—there are no billboards—but it is a legacy that will never be broken. He has poured his life into others, genuinely put others before himself, and never wants any credit for it. Ron has changed my life; he has been an absolute inspiration and helped me understand what *legacy* actually is.

People genuinely want to be liked by others, accepted by their peers, appreciated. It's human nature to seek approval, hence why people check social media sixty times per day on average. We want the "likes," we want more followers, because we want to feel important and appreciated. We all want to feel as if we are valued, and there is nothing wrong with that—we *should* feel the desire to be of value.

So, *create value.*

The true definition of legacy is living for the purpose we were created for and, in doing so, having a positive impact on one person. Yeah, that's right—just one.

If you live for a purpose, do what you are created to do, and make someone else's life better along the way, you will have left an admirable legacy. It might go unnoticed by society, but it will be a legacy that lasts longer than a lifetime. If you positively impact one person's life and they positively impact another person's life and the trend continues (which it will), think of the compounding interest your legacy will leave. One becomes millions. In making this *mindset pivot* from feeling like you have to be the next Martin Luther King Jr. to being content with positively impacting the lady at the grocery checkout counter every time you see her, or the secretary at your office who looks stressed out when you walk by every morning, you have the ability to change the world every single day.

Trust me, this mindset pivot is life-changing, and so is the impact you will have on others. You positively change one person's life, and you will be on their billboard *forever.*

SUCCESS

BLUEPRINT ACTION PLAN

1. Inside the heart, write down the five best parts of yourself and the ways you want to share them with the world every day. These aren't anything that would make a billboard—they're the very real ways you can make every day better for the people around you by being the best version of yourself.

For example, in my heart, I have these five pieces:

- Give out meaningful heartfelt compliments when I see something cool about someone.

- Make sure my (future) kids have the opportunity to follow their passion and the trust and comfort to know they can always be open with their mother and me by going out of my way to be the person that helps others pursue their passions and learning how to actively listen.

- Be so confident in my own skin it makes others confident in themselves.

- Have coffee, a smile, and a kiss ready every morning for my wife when she wakes up, so the first thing she sees every day is my unconditional love.

- Help improve everyone who reaches out to me with a passion for basketball so they can teach others down the road.

These are the things I'm committed to doing every day—and wow, what a legacy to leave!

2. Write down "MAKE A DIFFERENCE AND THE DIFFERENCE WILL MAKE YOU" on a notecard and place it on the dashboard of your car. Make the commitment to read it every time you get into your car, and every time you pass a billboard on the road, reflect on the true legacy you are building.

DAY 27
YOUNGER YOU

In June 2018, my good friend Casey Wasserman brought me on board at his sports agency (one of the largest and most powerful in the game) to coach all of their basketball clients in the off season and help them prepare for the upcoming year. I was in charge of sharpening the players' skills on court and their mindsets off court, helping them improve in all areas of their lives. I was essentially the life coach to twenty-three NBA players at one time. It was daunting, to say the least, making sure each of them got the attention and personalized coaching to help them improve and keep them happy and satisfied.

Three months into the job, I pulled over from my drive back to my Marina del Rey apartment one evening after nine hours straight on court for the fourth day in a row. My body ached and my mind was beyond fried. I was spent.

I sat down on a park bench overlooking the ocean and tried to find some peace and serenity. But all I could think was, "I still have two months left of this until the off season is over. Why do I have to work with so many players? This is miserable; my body can't take this anymore." I put my head in my hands, nearly in tears as I considered the road before me.

When I lifted my head up, I saw a dad and his son walking in the distance, hand in hand. The son dribbled a basketball, skipping as they walked. The dad kept stopping and getting down in a pretend defensive stance to guard the young boy, which made him laugh hysterically every time. If I were to guess, I would have said the boy was around eight years old.

Then it hit me: eight years old. The same age I was when I began shooting hoops in my basement for hours on end, pretending I was in the NBA, creating entire imaginary leagues, studying NBA players and everything about them, dreaming of the day that I would just *be around* the NBA. I lived and breathed anything I could get my hands on that had even the slightest thing to do with basketball. Forget button-down shirts or even t-shirts: for years, I wore a different NBA jersey each day. (I got a girlfriend in eighth grade, or I would have definitely continued the trend.)

Try to picture yourself at eight years old. Do you remember what you wanted to be when you grew up? Sure you do, we all do. We all had our dreams and our visions of our futures as astronauts, police officers, or in my case, as an NBA player. I dreamt about it day and night. The younger version of me would have killed to play, coach, or just watch as a fly on the wall.

Now I was, and I was complaining.

"What's wrong with me?" I literally asked aloud.

I had twenty-three high-level NBA players coming to me to help them improve their abilities, basically entrusting their livelihoods to my word. I was a mentor to them. I was living out what the *younger me* dreamed of—actually, to be honest, I was living out something *even cooler* and *more impressive*.

Younger me would have looked at current me on that Santa

Monica bench and been confused, ashamed, and disappointed: "David, this is what we dreamed of, this is more than we dreamed of!"

Eight-year-old David was right, and I knew it. It was all in my mindset. I was working with a "have-to" mentality instead of a "get-to" mentality. And that makes all the difference.

I told myself that night, "I don't *have to* train twenty-three elite NBA players, I GET TO." The mindset pivoted; *younger me* had reminded me how blessed and thankful I was to be living out my dream.

Why spend life not enjoying what you do? The time we have here on this earth is so fleeting, but so many of us get stuck in the "have-to" mentality. I know not all of us have the dream jobs our *younger selves* might have wanted, but there is something in all of our lives that we would have been extremely excited about. Not all of us acknowledge it. Myself included. Until that night.

When I was twenty-five years old with roughly $1,000 to my name (give or take $1,000), I had a decision to make: Do I continue to follow my passion for coaching, or do I go into commercial real estate, where the security and financial future was all lush green pastures?

During 7 AM pick-up basketball games in Palo Alto with billionaire VCs and Fortune 500 CEOs, I developed a relationship with one of the most powerful commercial real estate owners in the world. I hit the lottery when he offered me a job working under him until I could eventually become a partner—essentially guaranteed multi-millions within seven to ten years. Who wouldn't take that?

Everyone I talked to laughed when I told them the options I was weighing. "No-brainer," they all said. Why would anyone turn down guaranteed millions and a life of comfort for a barely-existent coaching business, running camps out of a beaten down Nissan Altima, driving all over the middle of nowhere Midwest with a bag of basketballs in the trunk?

As much as the world and those around me told me to go one way (commercial real estate), my heart told me there was no way I would be happy in a career of breaking down property measurements and doing deals I wasn't passionate about, no matter how lucrative the financial benefits were.

In a sweat-drenched t-shirt after pick-up basketball with the golden crew on the campus of Stanford University, I made a decision that I knew I might regret: I was going to live the life that I wanted to live and not care how anyone else wanted me to live it.

"I'm going to keep working on growing my basketball business," I told my high-power friend as we attempted to touch our toes after the game.

"You're making the right decision," my friend said clearly.

I was stunned.

He went on to tell me how he'd been faced with a decision early in his life to either take over the family business that had been passed down for generations, or to go against all *worldly* thinking and start his own commercial real estate company. Needless to say, he followed his heart, and his decision turned out pretty ok in the end.

Live the life everyone else really wants to live—the lives our eight-year-old-selves would have killed to live—without caring how anyone else wants to you to live it. Ultimately, everyone truly wants a life free of caring what others think, free of caring about what society *tells* them that they have to be. We all want our passion and joy to guide our decisions, not the tempestuous desire for money. Making those decisions can be extremely difficult, but on the days when you slip into "have-tos," straighten up and remind yourself that you *chose* to be where you are, and that your choice to pursue your passion was the right decision. Now you no longer "have-to," you GET TO!

BLUEPRINT ACTION PLAN

1. It's time to fill your younger you in on all the awesome stuff you've accomplished! Fill in the blank spaces to the right, and take a moment to think about how amazing your life now would seem if you could have seen it then!

2. Write down "LIVE THE LIFE I WANT WITHOUT CARING HOW ANYONE WANTS ME TO LIVE IT" on a notecard. If you have a child, place this notecard by your child's room. If you don't, put it by something in your home that reminds you of your childhood. (It could be a photo, a toy—anything that takes you back.) Commit to reflecting on how excited younger you would be by your life now and giving yourself a high-five each time you pass it.

Hey younger _____ , just wanted to
                    NAME

let you know that you have a _____
                              PERSON, THING

in your life that's the best, and also you get to

_____ every day. Turns out
THE COOLEST THING YOU DO

ice cream is not a viable breakfast option,

but otherwise, being an adult is pretty sweet.

Love, Future _____
                    NAME

DAY 28
CONGO TO HOLLYWOOD

HAVE YOU EVER FELT LIKE you were completely whiffing everything thrown your way? Like literally every potential opportunity that came up for you ended up going to someone else? You worked your butt off, every day putting in extra that you swore was going to pay off—and it didn't? What happens when all of the "relentless consistency," the "thriving over surviving" and "enjoying the daily grind" doesn't seem to actually pay off? What happens when you go through forty years of wandering in the wilderness only to wind up with nothing? Will you still prepare for the opportunity daily, like it could happen after forty years and one day? Or would you give in and feel sorry for yourself?

This story begins deep in the jungles of the Congo in Africa. In Lubumbashi, to be exact. Imagine living in this tiny copper mining town and walking forty-five minutes each day to get to school, without shoes. Once you get there, you have to ask friends for bites of their lunches, because your parents can't afford to feed you. This seems like a living nightmare, right? But this was the early life of NBA superstar Bismack Biyambo.

Bismack and I became fast friends in the summer of 2018. Like clockwork, we ran sprints on the Santa Monica beach at 7 AM, hit the basketball court to work on his skill development, and then followed that up with a powerful weightlifting session. More often than not, we were back on the court again in the evening for another basketball shooting session. (Trust me, I love the guy, but he WORE me out!)

About two months deep, I asked Bismack why he did what he did. After all, he'd just signed a deal with the Orlando Magic—$18 million per year for three years. The guy was set for life—multiple lives! I wanted to know what drove him to get out of bed every morning and work his butt off with such *relentless consistency*? I could tell it was how he was wired, but why?

Finally, I found out. And when I did, it suddenly all made sense.

Bismack's ticket out of his less-than-glamorous life in Africa was basketball. It was not only his ticket, but his entire family's best chance for survival. But what scout would ever come to the Congo to see Bismack play? If you answered "no one," you are correct.

At age sixteen, Bismack got his chance. Borrowing shoes from a friend, he set off incognito towards his destination: a basketball tournament in Qatar. The opportunity he had been preparing for was swept out from under him in Tanzania; Bismack was detained, arrested for leaving the Congo, and sent back. He was thrown in Congolese jail (Bismack says that people in prison in the United States have it good in comparison).

When he was released, he went right back to his training, working out for countless hours on nothing more than some yogurt he scrounged from a local market.

Nearly a year later, a basketball team from Yemen spotted Bismack and wanted him to come play in a tournament in Jordan.

PASSION

He knew this was the opportunity he had been preparing for. With papers in hand, Bismack flew to Jordan and showed them what he could do. And wow, did he show them! Bismack played like his life was on the line (which it basically was).

By sheer luck, a prolific European basketball scout happened to be in attendance that day. Dominating the game, Bismack caught the eye of the scout and was invited to play on a junior team in Spain.

Bismack took his *relentless consistency* and went to work, shredding the opposition each time he stepped on the floor. This led to an opportunity from the national team's head coach to play for one of the top pro teams in Spain. He wasn't even eighteen years old!

Bismack's ultimate breakthrough opportunity came when he was selected to represent the World Team in the prestigious Nike Hoop Summit in Portland, Oregon. Basically, if you play well in this game, you are guaranteed a spot in the NBA. All the miles back and forth to school, all the days he went without a meal, the time he spent locked away in that dingy jail, all of his blood, sweat, and tears—they all came down to this game. And Bismack was prepared for the opportunity that awaited him. Not only did he play well, he set the record as the first player to ever record a triple-double at the Summit (over 10 points, 10 rebounds, and 10 blocked shots).

The rest is history. Bismack went on to be chosen seventh overall in the NBA draft by the Charlotte Hornets. He has made upwards of $100 million over the span of his career, and provided for his family and the entire Congo—building hospitals, putting kids through school, feeding families, building shelters, and so much more. He uses his gift of basketball for the greater good of society, and positively impacts millions of lives. Bismack could have never done any of this if he hadn't been prepared for opportunity when it presented itself.

Let's just say I gained a better appreciation for dragging myself out of bed at the crack of dawn to run sprints on the beach.

Now I have to tell you about someone who really teaches me something about preparing for opportunity each and every day—the epitome of this mindset. Someone very near and dear to my heart. She, in fact, is my heart. My wife—my amazing, absolutely-out-of-this-world-blessed-to-have wife—Taylor Kalupa (Taylor Nurse when she's not acting, of course). She is my rock; she is the reason I am able to do what I do. She is also extremely talented in a business that is extremely unforgiving and can eat up even the strongest with stress, fear of the unknown, and worry for the future. She is an actress, a budding star in the industry. But acting jobs don't just happen. I've seen her prepare days, weeks, months for a role—just to be told, "Sorry, you're not the *exact* type we are looking for." Months of pouring your heart and soul into something without seeing the fruit of your labor, knowing that the part is out of your grasp forever? Yeah, that can be crushing—it would be *absolutely* crushing if she viewed each role or each opportunity as a single entity. Taylor doesn't. Taylor has learned that everything she does, every role she prepares for, whether she gets it or not, is preparation for a bigger opportunity to come.

In the acting industry, there is a season, from late January to early April each year, dedicated solely to casting TV show pilots. A pilot is the first episode of a potential TV series that networks pay to have filmed; based on how it turns out, they decide if they will film the rest of the season and air it on their channel. After going dry for four pilot seasons in a row, all of Taylor's preparation came through in a *big* break. Auditioning for an ABC pilot called *The Fix* (a primetime show written by Marcia Clark and based on the OJ Simpson trial), Taylor was so prepared that she blew them away. They gave her the part even with blonde hair, though the storyline called for an actress with brunette hair. (She dyed it brown for the show, of course!) But she crushed the audition! If she'd sulked and felt bad for herself after each rejection, each audition that she'd thought was the one, she would have never been fully ready to embrace that opportunity. And the pilot was picked up! It aired on national and international television on ABC, had billboards all over the country advertising it, and even had a promotion play during the Super Bowl.

Taylor is a constant inspiration to me, living proof that everything we do daily is a preparation for an opportunity to come. As her career continues to blossom and she becomes known all over the world, she will still experience rejection, still get turned down for roles, and still have doors slammed in her face. But what she knows, what I know, and now what you know as well, is that these "lost" opportunities are not lost at all—they are blocks building us up for our true opportunity. And when that opportunity comes, we will be so ready. We'll know we were *made* for the role—and everyone else will know it too. Your role of a lifetime is coming, trust me on that.

We all have something we are preparing for in our lives. We all have goals, visions, dreams of what we want to do and who we want to become. You might see others who haven't worked nearly as hard as you, who don't "deserve" to be more "successful" than you. You might feel like life isn't fair, like your opportunity will never come around. Your time might not come when you want it to. (Scratch that—it WON'T come exactly when you want it to.) But once you realize that things will happen on a different timeline and you'll wind up with even *greater* things than you expected, then everything you do in the "in between" will be purposeful and meaningful. The fruits of your labor will not shrivel up and prune; instead, they will flourish and blossom. If you believe that everything you do is *preparing for opportunity,* then no matter how long it takes for that opportunity to come, you will be ready. And when it comes, you will be so prepared that there will be no way for it to pass you by. You'll not only hit the ball hurtling at you—you'll knock it clear out of the park!

PASSION

BLUEPRINT ACTION PLAN

1. In the center of the clock, fill in an opportunity you'd love to have tomorrow—something big! If you knew it was going to come in twenty-four hours, how would you spend your time preparing today? At each quarter, write down one step you'd take to be ready.

   For example, I'd love to share my message to a sold-out stadium—but if I got the call that it would be waiting for me in just twenty-four hours, I would have a very busy day preparing! I'd spend the first quarter listening to motivational speakers who inspire me. For the second quarter, I'd reach out to everyone to invite them along! I'd spend the third quarter reworking my speech to make it just right. And fourth quarter, I'd practice it in front of my mirror, my wife, and anyone else who would listen!

   Look at your clock again and suppose you've got a year to prepare for this big opportunity. That feels a lot more manageable, doesn't it? Each of the things you've written in the quarter hours should be your focus over the next three months.

2. Write down "TREAT TODAY LIKE YOUR BIG OPPORTUNITY WILL BE TOMORROW" on a notecard and tape it to the last doorway you walk through to leave your home. Commit to preparing yourself for your big opportunity each time you step out into the world.

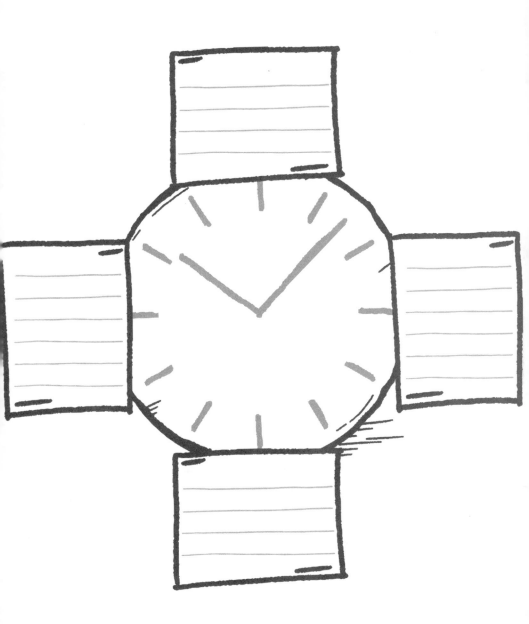

DAY 29+
RELENTLESS CONSISTENCY

I'M SURE YOU'VE HEARD ABOUT Malcolm Gladwell's idea that it takes 10,000 hours of deep learning to master a craft. That's a long time— 416.67 days straight, to be exact. The truth is, Gladwell is probably right—it takes AT LEAST 10,000 hours of deep, focused learning to become great at anything. And maybe even more. In a world obsessed with "lifehacks" and shortcuts (myself included), when it comes to complete mastery, there is no substitution for hard work itself.

At one time, I was considered one of the greatest basketball shooters in the world. I had a natural gift, but no one (except probably my mom) saw the hours it took to get there. I lived in the middle of nowhere, so I had that going for me—there really wasn't much else to do other than shoot hoops. I put in hours at the crack of dawn, evenings, and late into the middle of the night. I dragged my mother into the gym and made her rebound for me until her fingers bled. (Luckily, I have the best mom ever and she enjoyed that time with me, even if I was stern-faced and focused and didn't say a single word for five hours straight.) There were far, far too many days when I would do nothing besides shoot hoops until I couldn't feel my own fingers. I set out to be the best, and I made it. I set two world records in three point shooting and eventually became regarded as one of the top shooting coaches in the world.

Putting in the 10,000+ hours to become the best shooter in the world was great and all, but it wasn't substantial. It taught me that I had to put in hard work for what I wanted, but it didn't teach me the real meaning of *relentless consistency*. I found that out later in life—much later.

Ed Schilling is one of my best friends walking this planet. He even officiated my wedding. When we met, Ed was an assistant for UCLA Men's Basketball. UCLA had just been through one of their toughest years, and there was all kinds of pressure on the staff to rack up some wins or get the axe. Ed had a big family to support—two kids under the age of four and three older kids back home in Indiana. Ed also is a man of God, a mentor and a spiritual leader to over fifty people throughout the United States, who count on him daily to send a bible verse, word of encouragement, or just a check-in on the phone. He doesn't get paid a dime for that, but he does it anyways. Not just most days, but every day.

A typical day in the life of Ed Schilling included waking up at 5 AM, making his coffee, having his bowl of cereal, and diving into the Bible for the next hour, reading and writing in his journal like he had just discovered the secret of life. He would send out the morning Bible verse to each person in his network, myself included. Then, he'd go into his garage, where he had a pull-up bar and a broken-down old-school chest press machine, and he alternated each day between pull or push. Ed would workout, no matter if he felt like doing it or not, for fifteen to twenty minutes every single morning.

Ed would then go into the kitchen and make breakfast for his two daughters, which normally consisted of fruit, cereal, and extra crispy bacon. After this, he would take his four-year-old to pre-school, kiss his wife on the way out the door and ask if she needed him to pick up anything from the store that day or if there were any errands he could run. (Normally, his wife would do the errands, but Ed always offered.) He would then pack up his UCLA bag, drop his daughter off at school, battle LA traffic, and head to the office. All before 8:30 AM.

Meanwhile, seismic pressure was mounting on him and the UCLA staff—blimps flying over campus demanding the coaches be fired, and buses covered with billboards repeating the message. It was enough to make someone snap.

Now, you're probably thinking, "UCLA coach? I'm sure he's making more than enough money to get by. If he gets fired, he'll have enough to live off." Wrong. UCLA is an interesting university. It gives more credence to the idea of getting to be part of the university than it probably should. Ed lived paycheck to paycheck.

I would interact with Ed mostly at practice, with the occasional coffee or lunch to check in and ask him for mentorship (which he gave without ever asking anything in return).

College basketball tends to be a long season, and those daily practices can begin to wear on one's psyche. Not for Ed, though, or at least you would never know it. Every day at practice, Ed acted like he'd just consumed three Venti Starbucks with a shot of Red Bull. He would be bouncing off the walls with energy and positivity. If someone was having a noticeably bad day, Ed would be there to talk to them and pick them up. If anything needed to be taken care of—sweeping the floor, staying late to rebound for the players—Ed would do it with a smile.

I observed all of this, day after day, and took note of it. Why did he do everything every single day without asking for anything in return? I finally asked him one day after another late practice: "Ed, how do you have so much energy every day to give and serve everyone with a smile?"

He paused, looked me in the eye, and as if he was sharing one of life's most precious secrets (which he actually was), said, "Consistency. If people can't count on me to be consistent every day with who I am, no matter what the circumstances are, how are they ever going to be consistent in their own lives? If they see me complaining or taking days off from what I am here to do, how can I teach them how to be servants? How can I spread the love of Jesus with a servant-first mentality of consistency if I can't do it myself? David, everyone has things they are going through and things they are struggling with; I'm here to show them that no matter how hard things can get, the power of loving others can always reign supreme."

Wow. *Relentless consistency* to the max.

Ask yourself, are you someone that others would automatically recognize as consistent? Not through your words, but through your actions. Are you consistent in who you are, consistent in what you stand for, and consistent in loving others? Or are you like a chameleon that changes identity with its surrounding circumstances? One of my favorite Bible verses is 1 Thessalonians 5:18, "Give thanks in all circumstances." All circumstances, no matter great or trying, *all circumstances.* That is relentless consistency.

Can you rely on yourself consistently? Everything that we build, everything that we learn, everything that we become, and every mindset that we have pivoted will only turn into a real lifestyle change, a real *life* change, if we do them with *relentless consistency.*

Redefining Your Terms

Now that you've completed twenty-eight days and pivoted your mindset in life-changing directions, let's look back on those terms we talked about in the very beginning: **Success, Failure, Joy, Passion,** and **Confidence.** Do they mean something different to you now than when you started this book?

They should.

TRUE Success isn't tied to anything the world has to offer. It's knowing that we are living the life we were created to live. It's living each day with purpose, a sense of comfort that we know we are currently in this exact spot in life for a much bigger reason. Success is not about making a ton of money, being called an "influencer," or having any fleeting worldly possessions. It is ultimately loving your everyday life.

Success: living out each day to become more fully who you were made to be, knowing you are doing so for a much bigger purpose than yourself.

TRUE Failure is not a loss; it is a lesson. Failure is not a step back; it is an opportunity to learn. Failure is only negative if you get stuck in that rut. But if you look at failure as a gift to pivot to something so much better than your current situation, failure is a pathway to success.

Failure: potential losses or shortcomings that are perfect opportunities to learn, grow, and pivot.

TRUE Joy is an understanding that the extreme struggles and drastic changes you go through are all part of the adventure shaping you into who you were made to be. There is no end goal in life that is going to make us happy and not every day will be a wild adventure; life will be a grind at times. But joy is found in appreciating the process of those routines and habits. Every day is part of an exciting journey if we look at it knowing that it could be the best we'll ever have. Happiness is fleeting—joy is a choice.

Joy: a feeling of great pleasure and peace knowing that no matter what life throws your way, you are able to overcome it and fully enjoy the everyday life you live.

TRUE Passion is speaking into existence what it is you want to be and taking the daily steps on the path of life to reach that goal. We might have jobs we don't always like going to, but passion is knowing that we won't *always* have to be in those positions if we don't want to be. Passion is finding the best in your current situation and embracing it whole-heartedly.

Passion: learning to love what you do, not necessarily always doing what you love, all while enjoying the daily journey.

TRUE Confidence is being comfortable in your own skin no matter how *quirky* it might look to others. It is the knowledge that you have a gift from God specifically crafted and created for you. Confidence gives you the ability to step into any room and be completely, truly, genuinely, and fully yourself. You don't have to put on a mask, you don't have to try to be someone you're not; you can be fully yourself every single day.

Confidence: being fully comfortable in your own skin based on who you are—not what you do, not where you come from, but who you are on the inside.

Now that you have finished this book, you have all the tools in your hands to live every day better than the day before. It is here to help you set up your best life, your "rich" life, your "successful" life, your "ultimate" life, the life you have always wanted to live. That leap is no longer daunting—it's a simple pivot from where you currently are towards where you want to go.

I know that lifestyles definitely don't form overnight, or even over the course of however many days it took you to read this book. In order to create your dream lifestyle and make it an everyday reality, all it takes is a 1% step daily.

Some people still might think, "Well that's all great, but it's so daunting to consider changing my whole life or even just one aspect."

My response to that? I agree. That's why I just focus on one of the twenty-eight steps each day. For the first month, that's all you really need to do to get started. Take a calendar—whether it's a physical calendar or your cellphone calendar—and fill twenty-eight days out with the steps I've given you.

Those 10,000 hours it takes to become an expert? Well, think about this—if you dedicate twenty-four hours each month to just one of the mindset pivots in this book, and you do that a mere twelve days out of the year, you'll rack up 288 mastery hours. Now, multiply that by twenty-eight for all the steps I've given you—that equals 8,064. In just a little over a year, you will be an expert at the lifestyle I've shared with you. And that's only in ONE YEAR. That's so much more than just one skill set alone—you will have conquered an entire lifestyle. The lifestyle you have always dreamed about, the one you once thought was for the lucky, will now be your reality. And think about where you will be two years from now. Or even five. What about twenty? The potential you have to achieve YOUR success is literally LIMITLESS.

Your life is going to get better. It will go through peaks and valleys, of course, and it might even go through extended droughts. But over the long run, the lifestyle mindsets you have developed will compound on each other, to the point where you will look back years from now and wonder who you once were. It's happened to so many people I know personally, hundreds of high-level NBA players, Fortune 500 CEOs, and corporate business people. It's worked for me. These mindsets have pivoted me from stuck in a rut, living on my parents' recliner with only $132 to my name and no sense of purpose, to living the life I have always wanted, positively influencing people throughout the world, working with the top NBA players and professional athletes, traveling internationally to over fifty countries, and living out my PURPOSE, my PASSION, my MISSION, the reason I was put on this Earth. And it only gets better every day—all due to the mindset pivots I have outlined in this book, making small, simple changes daily that can change everything.

Today is your day. The life you have always wanted to live starts now. The choice is yours.

ACKNOWLEDGMENTS

FIRST AND FOREMOST I WANT to thank God, to whom I owe everything. He has blessed me beyond my wildest dreams and has gifted me a mission to serve others and show them what true joy is.

My amazing wife Taylor. She is my rock, my biggest supporter, my best friend, the love of my life, literally in every way my everything. Without her there is NO WAY this book would be what it is and NO WAY I would be who I am.

My parents Ann and Dan. For raising me to be the person I am today and always believing I could do anything I set my mind to. No matter how crazy it sounded they were always there supporting me and cheering me on every step of the way.

My brother Paul and my sister Julia. For helping to show me what it is like to live for Christ and for the countless hours spent dreaming and imagining together.

The Mascot family: To Naren, for believing in me and taking the leap of faith believing an NBA coach could become an author. Lauren, for editing and shaping this book to be what it is, and of course putting up with me the entire way.

Nick Nurse. Even through the ups and downs he has always been there for me and taught me countless invaluable life lessons.

All NBA players mentioned in this book and some of my best friends on this planet:

Jeremy Lin, Aron Baynes, Kelly Olynyk, Bismack Biyambo, Domas Sabonis, Kyle Korver, Joe Johnson, and Tom Welsh.

And all NBA players who have put their trust in me and allowed me to help shape their lives.

You guys are more than just friends, you are brothers.

Mark Dyer and Roger Fields. For making this dream a reality and being the most supportive friends I could have!

To all of my mentors throughout this journey who have shown me the way:

Ron Adams

Erik Spoelstra

Jeff Jordan

Gary Sacks

Steve Thorne

Ed Schilling

To my non-blood related 'families' who have always taken me in:

Steve Alford and family

Casey Wasserman and family

Kris and Neda Weems for the guest room, where it all began.

Ted. My friend and a huge inspiration for writing this book.

To all my family throughout the world who have taken me in and offered me a couch and a warm meal.

And to everyone who has ever believed in me. Everyone who has ever encouraged me. Everyone who has ever spoken life into me.

Thank you, I am forever grateful.

ABOUT THE AUTHOR

David Nurse is an NBA life and optimization coach, future bestselling author, and worldwide motivational speaker.

As a former domestic and international professional basketball player and coach for the Brooklyn Nets, David has helped more than 150 NBA players with their personal and professional development both on and off the court. He has been invited to speak in more than 50 different countries on the topics of overall personal development, confidence building, leadership, and motivational growth.

David resides in Marina del Rey, California, and is married to the love of his life, the stunning actress Taylor Kalupa.